GIDEON
A HERO IN THE MAKING

GIDEON
A Hero In the Making

DR. F. BRUCE WILLIAMS

DEDICATION

This book is dedicated to the heroes and heroines who have poured into my life in meaningful ways:

To my hero and father, Rev. Earl B. Williams who showed me the heart of a pastor and taught me to never give up! To my heroine and mother, Norrine T. Williams who breathed in me the belief that I could do anything God had called me to do.

To the heroes that mentor(ed) me: Rev. Larry Hunt, Rev. C. C. Cunningham, Rev. Dr. Ronald Bobo, Rev. Dr. Jeremiah Wright and Dr. Jawanza Kunjufu.

To my heroine in life, love, marriage and ministry, my best friend and lover, L. Michelle Williams who sustained me through the darkest times and daily inspires me to be the man, husband, father, pastor, preacher, friend and servant God is calling me to be. Michelle, aside from God, you are my primary motivation to achieve. I love you.

To my little heroines, my lovely daughters Imani and Nailah. There is a call on both of your lives. Be fearless and rise to your calling.

To that village full of heroes and heroines, Bates Memorial Baptist Church, who dream with me and are busy about the business of doing the work of the Kingdom; my life is richer, the Kingdom is bigger and the world is better because of you.

Finally, to those of you who may not have discovered that you are indeed heroes and heroines in the Lord—may the Lord open your eyes so that you may see *you* the way God sees *you*.

~Dr. F. Bruce Williams

TABLE OF CONTENTS

ACKNOWLEDGEMENTS

First and foremost I want to thank God for choosing me to serve and for giving me a passion to show the "least of these" that there is greatness even in them.

I want to thank the wonderful and dedicated staff and members of Bates Memorial Baptist Church for believing in me and giving me space to stretch myself and use all of my gifts to be a blessing to others for the sake of the Kingdom.

A special thanks to my Administrative Assistant, Hannah Drake (who is also resident poet and author). I am forever indebted to you for not only being so conscientious about "organizing my life" so that I can do what God has spoken in my heart to do, but also for your constant encouragement regarding the writing ministry God has in me.

Thanks to Miriam Williams, a faithful disciple at Bates Memorial and gifted writer, for her valuable contribution in editing the manuscript for the final copy.

I also want to say a great big 'thank you' to Francis Middleton, a faithful member of Bates Memorial, for asking me time and time again, "When are you going to write the book?" Well Sister Middleton, here is one of them!

I certainly want to thank my dear wife Michelle from the bottom of my heart for believing in me enough to constantly and patiently encourage me to reach toward my full potential! You are my everything.

May the Lord bless you all for helping to make this book a reality.

~Dr. F. Bruce Williams

INTRODUCTION

I can remember from the time I was a young boy thinking that I wanted to do something great with my life. In fact, more accurately, I believed that I *would* do something great with my life. I believed that I was destined to do something meaningful. What that 'great thing' was I did not know. But as I grew, I dreamed of pursuing a varied assortment of career paths, and fantasized about making positive contributions and enjoying meaningful accomplishments. I have a feeling that most children start out with that spark, that something that makes them dream of doing something great. Unfortunately, for so many of us, life, circumstances, disappointments, crisis, fear or just plain boredom cause us to settle for doing something less than great.

We end up thinking that we can never make a difference. We conclude that we will never do anything meaningful for the uplifting of others or ourselves. So we settle for a mediocre life of just going through the motions. Even worse, we spend our lives watching others live with meaningful purpose, while our lives merely meander along.

But God never intended for your life to be meaningless and without purpose. God created you to make your contribution by rising to the heights that God has above you and living up to the best that God has in you. God has a hero in you.

As a child of God there is so much the Master has for you to do, so many things worthwhile to participate in. Think about it—in Jesus' name there are souls to save, families to strengthen, the hungry to feed, the naked to clothe, the homeless to house, the oppressed to liberate, the downtrodden to encourage, institutions to build, dilapidated homes to renovate, drug infested neighborhoods to clean, hearts to encourage, broken lives to make whole, disease to heal, cures to discover, businesses to start, children to rear and educate, prisoners to visit and encourage, love to share, a gospel to preach, a difference to make, schools to enhance, degrees to earn, books to write, evil to challenge, justice to establish, institutions to build, churches to enhance, a cross to bear, a life to live, a death to die and a God to glorify! And God wants to use you to make a powerful and positive difference. You can do something that matters in time and towards eternity if you will let God bring out the hero in you! In fact, right now, you might be "a hero in the making."

Some say that heroes are born and not made. Others argue that heroes are made and not born. I suspect that both claims are correct. Heroes are both born and made. I believe that each of us is born having within us the stuff of which heroes are made. And, as we are put in the fires of human tests and trials, that 'stuff' can be developed by God who can then take us and make us the heroes God intends for us to be.

This series of sermons investigates the life of a man named Gideon. At first blush Gideon seems a most unlikely hero. But as we witness his encounter with God and his subsequent career, we see how God carefully, skillfully, patiently and miraculously makes and molds this man into the hero God intended him to be and into the hero his nation sorely needed. And in so doing, Gideon becomes an example of what God can do with the humblest of human souls.

This work is not only about how God can use a person to make a difference but how God can use the church to make a difference. In the African American community, the church has historically been, in many ways, a priestly and prophetic institution that has been a place to find spiritual succor in Christ, to compassionately minister to human need and prophetically challenge the nation to live up to its highest ideals. For me, the church is still the best place in town. At its best the church is still the most significant institution, save the family. So this book of sermons intends to inspire the church and the people of God to rise up and be the hero that God intends for the church to be as well.

As a pastor/preacher my inclination is to prepare sermons for the ear and not the eye. I was initially apprehensive about publishing this series of sermons because I was afraid that the impact of the sermons would be lost in their journey from the audio to the visual; from the spoken word to the written word. Whether that happens or not remains to be seen. I only hope that you, the reader, will not be the loser. My prayer is that this series of sermons will somehow inspire you to trust your life to God in Christ and to discover the hero in you.

CHAPTER 1

A HERO IN THE MAKING

[1] Again the Israelites did evil in the eyes of the LORD, and for seven years he gave them into the hands of the Midianites. [6] Midian so impoverished the Israelites that they cried out to the LORD for help. [7] When the Israelites cried to the LORD because of Midian, [8] he sent them a prophet, who said, "This is what the LORD, the God of Israel, says: I brought you up out of Egypt, out of the land of slavery. [9] I snatched you from the power of Egypt and from the hand of all your oppressors. I drove them from before you and gave you their land. [10] I said to you, 'I am the LORD your God; do not worship the gods of the Amorites, in whose land you live.' But you have not listened to me." [11] The angel of the LORD came and sat down under the oak in Ophrah that belonged to Joash the Abiezrite, where his son Gideon was threshing wheat in a winepress to keep it from the Midianites. [12] When the angel of the LORD appeared to Gideon, he said, "The LORD is with you, mighty warrior." [13] "But sir," Gideon replied, "if the LORD is with us, why has all this happened to us? Where are all his wonders that our fathers told us about when they said, 'Did not the LORD bring us up out of Egypt?' But now the LORD has abandoned us and put us into the hand of Midian." [14] The LORD turned to him and said, "Go in the strength you have and save Israel out of Midian's hand. Am I not sending you?" [15] "But Lord," Gideon asked, "how can I save Israel? My clan is the weakest in Manasseh, and I am the least in my family." [16] The LORD answered, "I will be with you, and you will strike down all the Midianites together."

(Judges 6:1; 6-16 NIV84)

God has a way of choosing the most unlikely people from the most unlikely places to do great things. It is amazing where God finds heroes to do his bidding. Now, it is true that heroes and heroines sometimes come from the ranks of the powerful and the privileged. There are many who are considered to be among society's elite that God has inspired to do great things on God's behalf. All privileged are not pampered. All those who are socially successful are not selfish and self centered. There are many who have both great cash flow and great compassion. There are those who are among the prosperous and prestigious who are sensitive to the plight of others and understand that 'to whom much is given much is required.'

But the Bible says that God has this holy habit of using the foolish things of this world to shame the wise and the weak things to shame the strong. (1 Corinthians 1:27) God does that to humble us. God does it so that we can realize that without him we are nothing. God does that to let us know that it is really about him. God does that to teach us that no matter who we are, God can use us. It is not your rank or race, group, gifts or gender, age or assets that qualify you to be used by God. God uses the most unlikely people, from the most unlikely places, in the most pitiful predicaments to do great things because he wants us to learn that He is the key and that it is not our ability but our availability that makes us hero material.

In our text God does something great with a most unlikely person. He develops a leader from the least of these, takes a nobody and makes him a somebody, chooses a zero and makes him a hero and as a consequence sets a people free. It happened during the time of the Judges. The time of the Judges was a 350-odd year period between the time that Joshua brought Israel into the Promised Land until the time that Israel got her first king, King Saul. During that time Israel's relationship with God was characterized by a reoccurring cycle of deliverance and disobedience. God would send a judge or deliverer to lead the people. While that leader was alive the people would enjoy great peace and prosperity. But, once that leader died the people of God would begin to adopt the ways of the surrounding nations and would become guilty of the very things that God had warned them against. Down, down, down into immorality they would descend until Israel's disobedience to God led to humiliating oppression by their enemies.

After a period of humiliation and devastation, the people of God would then cry out to God for help and even though it was their own sins that had put them in their predicament, God in His magnanimous nature and limitless love would hear their cry and come to their rescue by raising up a judge who would deliver them from the consequences of their misbehavior. As that judge began to reign, the nation would experience another great period of prosperity and peace. But once that judge died, the cycle of sin would begin all over again.

That's where our text begins. Once the judge, Deborah, that great military strategist, that powerful prophetess and deliverer of God's people had died as other judges before her, chapter six verse one reports that once again the children of Israel did evil in the sight of God.

This time their disobedience led to their being oppressed by the Midianites. First, the Midianites attacked the Israelites' community and caused them to flee in fear from the place of their habitation up to the hills to live in caves like animals. Then, to add insult to injury, when the harvest time came, the enemy would descend on them like locusts and devour what the Israelites worked hard to produce. They would also steal their livestock, cattle, sheep and their donkeys and once they were finished, they would disappear as quickly as they had come, waiting for the next harvest to steal again.

It is worth noting that even now as believers in Christ, we have an enemy. And this enemy is not satisfied with you simply living in fear. The enemy wants to devour what God intends to use to bless you. The enemy wants to devour your health, your home, your relationships, your sustenance, your finances, your hopes, your dreams, your vision, your joy and your peace of mind. If like Israel in the text, you let the enemy in by way of personal persistent disobedience, the enemy's goal is to bring nothing short of devastation, humiliation, bondage and destruction.

The enemy came in and devoured the Israelites' goods - the very goods that God intended for them to enjoy - and left them depressed, despondent and devastated. This went on every year for seven years straight. Then Israel cried out for help. But Israel did not ask for help from the Assyrians, mighty Babylon or the Egyptians. Israel cried out to the God whom they had abandoned and offended. And the Lord heard their cry and came to their rescue.

Isn't that amazing? Israel had forsaken God but in their hour of despair God did not forsake them. That's good news because whatever else that means, it means that if you are a victim of the consequences of your own persistent disobedience and the enemy is trying to make you believe that there is no help from heaven for you, please understand that if you just look up and cry out to the Lord in sincere repentance, God is so gracious and merciful that God will come and see about you!

The text reports that God came to the rescue of Israel. No wonder John writes in 1 John 4:8 that God is love. Only God will come to the rescue of people who are being hardheaded, hard-hearted and stiff-necked. Our loving and merciful God came to their rescue.

A Prelude to Deliverance: God Sent A Prophet

Notice how God initially responded to their cry for help. Verses 7 - 10 reveal first that "God sent a prophet." Now the text doesn't name the prophet. We don't know anything about this prophet. We don't know anything about his history, or his heritage. We don't know where he came from or where he went after he preached. We don't learn anything about his family or his credentials. We only learn that he is a prophet sent by God.

Furthermore, the text says that this unknown, unnamed prophet came and gave Israel a word from the Lord. He began to bring up their history with God. He says in substance, "Now you know it was God who brought you out of Egyptian bondage. You know it was God who brought you safely through the wilderness, across the Red Sea and into the Promised Land. You know it was God who gave you the power to advance and made your enemy give up land so you could live in houses you did not build and eat from olive trees you did not plant. You know it is God who sustains you and told you not to fear the idol gods of this surrounding nation. And yet, He says you would not hear Him. You have disobeyed Him."

Now, there are a few things I want you to see regarding this prophet. First, this prophet is unnamed. He remains unnamed because God wants to make a point. What is important about the prophet is not *who* the prophet is, but *what* the prophet says. This prophet is nothing but an ambassador for the Lord. His identity is not that important. An ambassador does not get his power from himself but from the one whom the ambassador represents.

We who are called to proclaim God's word must remember that we are just representatives. In fact, Dr.

Mack King Carter, Pastor Emeritus of Mount Olive Baptist Church in Fort Lauderdale, Florida refers to preachers as "delivery boys or mailmen." And in a real sense that's all we are. We are men and women who deliver divine mail. Our identity is not that pivotal. God uses us but God doesn't need us. Whenever we who preach get to the point where we think God can't do what God wants to do without us, then we are thinking more highly of ourselves than we ought! What is most important about it is not who we are, but who sent us and the message we must deliver!

The second thing I want to point out is that the unnamed prophet speaks a word from the Lord. This is paramount. That is what makes the prophet important. It's not so much who the prophet is, but rather whether the prophet faithfully delivers the mail or preaches God's Word. It's important that the prophet faithfully delivers God's word because the Word of God is Truth and it is still true that the Truth can set you free! The prophet came, the prophet preached and then the prophet left. And oftentimes the prelude to your deliverance is that God will stop and drop His word on you and leave you with Truth that can change your life!

The Word that the prophet delivers is a Word that was a reminder to the people that the God whom they were calling on, the God whom they had deserted and disobeyed, is the same God who had chosen and blessed them in the first place. This was an important reminder to the people as they prepared to be delivered. There are times in our lives when we turn our backs on God because we forget how good God has been to us. We forget that it is God who keeps us, blesses us, cares for us and provides for us. And in those seasons when we begin to forget, it is then that we can become candidates for ingratitude and disobedience. From time to time it would do us well to remember that we owe the enemy nothing but we owe God everything. The enemy means us no good but what God desires for us is only good!

Looking For a Deliverer

In answer to the cry of the people God started looking for a deliverer. Now deliverance did not come immediately but God was at work bringing it to pass. This serves as a reminder that when you cry out to God for help, you may not see immediate evidence of your deliverance but that doesn't mean that God is inactive. Just because you can't see what God is doing doesn't mean that God isn't doing anything. Just because you don't know what God is doing doesn't mean that God doesn't have a plan. Just because you can't see how deliverance can come doesn't mean that God can't deliver. Don't ever think that just because you don't see it and can't understand it that God can't do it! God is busy preparing what you need in order for you to be delivered. In fact, while Israel was crying out to God for deliverance, God sent an angel down to an unlikely place to talk to an unlikely man. The angel showed up at a village called Ophrah and sat under an oak tree belonging to Joash of the clan of Abiezer. There Joash's son, a man named Gideon, was threshing wheat in a wine press.

Now, that's strange when you think about it. Gideon was threshing *wheat* at a *winepress*. You don't thresh wheat at a winepress. You're supposed to make wine at a winepress. What is Gideon doing threshing wheat in a winepress? The Bible reports that he was threshing wheat at a winepress because he was hiding. And he was hiding because he was *afraid*. His fear caused him to thresh wheat at a winepress so that the Midianites couldn't find him.

Sin can lead to fear and fear can lead to hiding. When you are dominated by fear, if you are not careful, you'll find yourself doing strange things in unusual places. Gideon was threshing wheat in a winepress and no doubt his heart was heavy. He felt discouraged, defeated and like his people, Gideon felt the devastating humiliation of being oppressed by a weaker nation. But things were about to change.

Where is the Lord?

When the angel showed up, the angel greeted Gideon by declaring, "The Lord is with you, you mighty warrior." The first part of that greeting was simply a standard greeting. The angel looked at Gideon threshing wheat in a winepress and said, "The Lord is with you." That's like saying "good morning." That's like saying "hello." But the angel added to the standard greeting this phrase "...you mighty warrior." Now that seems a rather extravagant title for a scared man secretly threshing wheat at a winepress. It didn't seem like the Lord was with him and he sure didn't look like a "mighty warrior."

It is clear that Gideon is not impressed with the salutation. He immediately responds by saying in substance, "What do you mean the Lord is with me? Where is the Lord?" You know how, when you're having a bad day or you feel like you're having a bad life and somebody comes to you and says, "Good morning!" and you stop and say, "What's so good about it?" Well, that's what Gideon was doing. The angel says, "The Lord is with you" and Gideon says, "Well, where is the Lord? If the Lord is with us, then why are all of these terrible things happening to us? And why are there no more miracles like our fathers spoke of?"

At this point in the encounter it is clear that Gideon had a heart that no longer had much hope. How can we know this? First of all Gideon believed that God was absent. He believed that God was not with them or for them. And there's nothing that will make a person sit down and give up like the feeling that God is absent. Have you ever been there?

Not only did he feel that God was absent, but he also decided that the evidence of God's absence was the absence of miracles. Gideon complained, "Where are the miracles that our fathers spoke of?" He said that because he understood that the only one who could get them out of their predicament was God and the only thing that could change their circumstances was a miracle. One thing that can take the wind out of the sails of your determination and make your hope go on vacation is when you believe that God is absent and that God's power is unavailable. That will make you thresh wheat at a winepress won't it? It can cause you to live in fear, defeat and despair.

Gideon was asking, "Where is God? Why is all of this happening to us? Where are the miracles that our fathers spoke of? They testified about our people being miraculously delivered from Egyptian bondage; about seas splitting, bread falling from heaven and rivers rolling up on either side. Where are the miracles that our fathers spoke of? If we've ever needed a miracle we need them now!" Perhaps you have been in a situation where you have felt just like this. It seems like the bottom has fallen out of your life and it seems like God is on vacation. You remember hearing the preacher declare or your grandmother testify or your parents teach that God is able, that God is a deliverer, that God can do anything but fail. In better days you believed it too. But now that all hell has broken loose in your life and you have felt the hellish consequences for a long time with no apparent relief on the horizon, you start to wonder "Where is God? And where are the miracles that

I heard so many people I trust testify about?" You hate to admit it, but the situation has drained you of almost every ounce of faith you have. You have all but given up on God and have been reduced to threshing wheat at a winepress.

But notice that even though Gideon's response is full of frustration and faithlessness, Gideon's lack of faith does not put that angel in an adversarial relationship with Gideon. Instead, the text reports that the angel responded to Gideon's frustration by saying "Go in the strength you have and save Israel out of Midian's hand. Am I not sending you?"

You are the Answer!

After Gideon complained about the predicament of his people by saying in substance, "Do you see how bad off we are? Where is God? Where are the miracles? Where is the deliverer?" the angel pointed at Gideon and said, "There he is! You ask 'where is the answer?' Well, YOU are the answer. Where is the deliverer? YOU are the deliverer!"

Sometimes when you can see something to complain about maybe it's because you are the answer for what you are complaining about. If things are not as they ought to be in your home, family, finances, physical health, neighborhood, schools, government, city, church or life, and all you can do is complain because nobody seems to be doing anything about it, maybe you're the answer to what your complaining about! Maybe God is calling on you!

All along God was saying-*Gideon, you're the answer!* YOU deliver my people!

"Go in the strength you have and save Israel out of Midian's hand. Am I not sending you?"

"Go in the strength you have..." What strength? I believe that God was saying through the angel to Gideon that the strength he would need for the task is found in the fact that *God was sending him*. What a word! I am confident that Gideon did not see within himself anything equal to the call that God was challenging him to embrace. But God was letting Gideon know that the strength he needed was in the God who sent him.

What about you? Do you realize that God is calling you to do something? Perhaps you are afraid to take up the task because you realize that you are inadequate for the task. Well, if God is calling you, let this be your strength...it is God who is calling you! And whatever you need, God will supply. And whatever you are not, God can make up the difference.

No Excuses

Once the angel articulated the call to Gideon, Gideon began to hesitate. He started to make excuses like Moses did ("I am not a good speaker"), like Jeremiah did ("I am but a child"), like Isaiah did ("I am a man of unclean lips and I dwell among a people of unclean lips"), like a host of people did in the past and still do now *"I can't go! What do you mean? I thought you were going to choose somebody else; not me! Let me tell you angel why I can't go. I've got a good reason why I can't go."*

Have you ever been there? Have you ever talked to God like that? Have you ever said, "Not me! I can't do it! And I've got some good reasons why I can't do it." Consider what Gideon said: *"I can't go because after all, I'm a part of a tribe that's the least tribe in all of Israel."* He continued, *"And if that's not bad enough, not only am I a member of the least tribe in all 12 tribes of Israel, but I'm the least one in the least tribe in the least family in all of Israel."*

In other words, Gideon was saying "I can't go because I'm the least of the least. I can't go because of my family background. I'm not related to anyone significant.

There is no one famous in my family. No one in my clan has ever been to school. They have never accomplished anything great. They've never had their picture on the front of *Time Magazine.* There's nobody special in my family. I don't come from any extraordinary stock. There's nothing that anybody can brag about in my family. I can't go. I can't do it. I can't accomplish it. I can't start that business, graduate from college, learn a new skill, teach any students, stand up for myself, stand up for what's right, speak truth to power, kick this bad habit, overcome this addiction, make any meaningful contribution or really make a difference— not ME!

And sometimes what causes us to sit down instead of stand up, step back instead of step up, sit still instead of move forward; serve ourselves instead of serving others; make excuses instead of making plans, do nothing instead of doing something, is that we come from a certain kind of family, are tied to a certain type of history, and believe that we are therefore destined to repeat what has come before us. But you don't have to be defined by what others in your family have done before you. You may have had an alcoholic daddy and a crack addicted mama, but that does not mean that has to be your destiny. Your family may have been poor all of their lives, and may have never been a part of a church. They may have never gone to college, never thought that their lives mattered, never reached for anything better, never taken a risk for the sake of good or never tried or cared to make a difference with their lives. They may have never cared anything about God, Christ or doing right, but just because they were that way does not mean that you have to be that way.

You may come from the poorest zip code in your area, but don't you dare be defined by where you came from. Where you came from doesn't determine who you are or where you're headed. That's why the angel said to Gideon—a defeated and frightened man threshing wheat in a winepress— "mighty warrior." The angel said that because God doesn't just look at who you are, but at who you can become, not just where you've been, but where you want to go. God doesn't simply see who you are presently, God sees who you are potentially! God created you and knows all about you. God knows that you are greater than what has happened to you, where you come from and even the negative circumstances that you may be in right now!

Don't you know that God is in the business of making heroes? Consider Peter in the New Testament. The

Bible reports in John chapter one that when Jesus looked at Simon he said, "You are Simon but you shall be called Cephas." Cephas means Peter or rock. So Jesus says, "You are Simon, but shall become a rock." Jesus was saying in substance to Simon that "You are what you are now, but you shall become what I'm going to make you—a rock."

And that's what I like about God. Even though God will meet you where you are, God won't leave you where God found you. You may be what you are right now but under the tutelage of the Almighty you can become something greater than what you are. So stop using excuses like, "That's just the way I am." Don't you know that God is in the business of giving you power so that you might become more than what you have made of yourself?

That's why one of my favorite scriptures is John 1:12 KJV: "But to as many as received Him, to them gave He power to become the sons of God." In other words, if you receive Jesus, He gives you power to *become*. You can't become what you ought to become on your own because there's really no such thing as a self-made person. A self-made person is a self-made mess because the best we can do is imperfect at best. But, if you want power to *become,* the Bible says if you receive Jesus, God can give you power to become what God intends for you to become.

So come on mighty warrior! Come on my sister, come on my brother. I know you're afraid. I know you don't have much confidence in your history. I know you don't even have much confidence in yourself. But stop threshing wheat at a winepress. Stop settling for less than what God has destined and designed for you. That isn't what God wants you to do all of your life. God has a greater destiny than you threshing wheat at a winepress, hiding out behind excuses, living in fear, living below your privilege. God wants to make your life count for something greater than just going through the motions. If you've settled for less than what God wants for your life; if you're satisfied with living in fear and making excuses for why you will never amount to anything, then God is trying to tell you that God's got a greater future, a nobler way of living, a higher destiny for you! God doesn't want you to live in fear. God has a hero in you!

CHAPTER 2
TEAR IT DOWN

²⁵ *That same night the LORD said to him, "Take the second bull from your father's herd, the one seven years old. Tear down your father's altar to Baal and cut down the Asherah pole^M beside it.* ²⁶ *Then build a proper kind of altar to the LORD your God on the top of this height. Using the wood of the Asherah pole that you cut down, offer the second bull as a burnt offering."* ²⁷ *So Gideon took ten of his servants and did as the LORD told him. But because he was afraid of his family and the townspeople, he did it at night rather than in the daytime.* ²⁸ *In the morning when the people of the town got up, there was Baal's altar, demolished, with the Asherah pole beside it cut down and the second bull sacrificed on the newly built altar!* ²⁹ *They asked each other, "Who did this?" When they carefully investigated, they were told, "Gideon son of Joash did it."* ³⁰ *The people of the town demanded of Joash, "Bring out your son. He must die, because he has broken down Baal's altar and cut down the Asherah pole beside it."* ³¹ *But Joash replied to the hostile crowd around him, "Are you going to plead Baal's cause? Are you trying to save him? Whoever fights for him shall be put to death by morning! If Baal really is a*

god, he can defend himself when someone breaks down his altar."

(Judges 6: 25-31, NIV)

In our world there are often personal pain and perplexing problems. In the midst of these realities, it is not unusual to hear Christian believers say that they are looking for God to break through and make a difference. And, if anybody can make a difference, surely God can.

But as I examined this story of God's encounter with Gideon and Gideon's reply to God, I am reminded of a profoundly challenging truth. While we are lamenting this world looking for God to make a difference, God is also lamenting this world and looking for us to make a difference. While we are waiting for God to break in and change the circumstances, God is waiting on us to stand up and rise to the occasion. While we're busy looking up to heaven asking God, *"Why don't you do something?"* God is looking down from heaven asking, *"Well, why don't you help me?"*

So, you're tired of the way things are. You're tired of your present circumstances. You're tired of the persisting problems. You're tired of that depression. You're tired of those self defeating habits and issues. You hate your situation, you don't like your plight, you despise your predicament and you want to be free. Well, things don't have to stay the way they are! That's right! You don't have to stay where you are and things don't have to stay the way they are. God says deliverance can be yours on one condition: **You have got to be willing to participate in your own deliverance!**

Gideon did not want to live in fear and defeat. But When God met Gideon, God did not tell Gideon "I will go *for* you." God said, "I will go *with* you." He was saying to Gideon that they were in it together! Gideon would have to participate in his own deliverance.

And herein lies the answer to many of our situations. Oftentimes the reason why an undesirable situation persists in our lives is because **we won't participate in our own deliverance.** We want to be free but won't participate in our own deliverance. We want to be blessed by God, but we refuse to trust and obey God. We want our financial needs met, but we won't manage our money according to kingdom principles and sound financial management. We want better relationships, but we refuse to leave those old oppressive relationships alone. We want to be strong in faith, but we won't get where we can hear God's Word. We want to hear from God, but we won't pray. We want to receive, but we don't want to give. We want to be forgiven, but we won't forgive. We want justice, but we won't fight for it. We want the promotion on the job, but we come late and leave early. We want to be delivered from ignorance, but we are too lazy to read a good book. We want better neighborhoods, schools, churches, families, marriages and businesses, but we are not willing to put in the time, effort and sacrifice to make them better. We want things to change, but we keep on doing the same old thing. We want to be free, but we want God to deliver us while we're reclining in our easy chair with the spiritual remote control in our hands. We want the work to be done, but we want God to do it all by God's self. But God didn't say, "I will go *for* you!" God says, "I will go *with* you." God said, "If you want to be delivered, well, come on! Let's do it together."

Start At Your House

Now, if I was to take God's strategy given to Gideon and reduce it down to its irreducible essence, God says to

Gideon, "If you want to be delivered, you've got to do the following: Tear it down *and* build it up."

First, God says, "Gideon, tear it down." Tear down what? Tear down the altars of Baal. Tear down those idols. That was the problem. *Idolatry* was the problem. They had given up on God with a big "G" and started serving gods with a little "g". And God said, in substance, that as long as those altars and idols are up, no deliverance is forthcoming. But, I'm not coming down from heaven to tear them down. God says to Gideon, "You tear down those idols."

Did you know that in order to be delivered there are some things that God is not going to do for you? There is a part that God is going to do. And believe me, you never have to worry about whether God will do God's part. But there is a part that you are required to do. And even though God is omnipotent, even though God has all power, there are some things that God will not do for you. If it's going to get done, YOU ARE GOING TO HAVE TO DO IT. Those idols that God referred to were idols that God was not going to get rid of. In a real sense, God was saying to Gideon, "In order for me to know that you are serious about deliverance YOU are going to have to get rid of those idols. You put them there, you remove them." And in order for certain things to happen in your life, God is declaring that you are going to have to set it right. You brought it in (or allowed it in) your life, you are going to have to repent, renounce and remove it. YOU tear it down.

Or perhaps you didn't put it in your life. Perhaps there is something in your life that has become an idol that initially was forced on you. There is something negative that has happened in your life that you have ascribed so much power to that for all practical purposes it has become like a god. It has taken control of your life. In fact, you really want it out of your life. Or you want the negative influence it is having out of your life. The way it makes you feel about yourself is getting in the way of what you want to do with your life. Well, believe it or not, it does not have to continue to dominate you and intimidate you. God is saying right now that it's not really a god, it's an imposter. You have God's permission to tear it down!

I want you to notice something. When God told Gideon to tear them down, the first place that Gideon had to go was where he lived. Gideon was a young man. He was not yet on his own so Gideon was living at his daddy's house. So, when God said, "Tear down the altars of Baal at your daddy's house," the first place Gideon had to start was at his own house.

Sometimes, if you want things to be better around you, you have to start with you. If you want things to be better in your church, community, neighborhood, city, state, country and the world, understand that it all starts first at your house! First, get rid of the idols at your house! Often the prelude to deliverance, blessings and a brand new start, is to start at our own house. Stop spending so much time and energy trying to fix someone else somewhere else. Jesus said, "Why are you trying to remove the speck out of your brother's eye when you've got this big two-by-four in your own eye? First extract the big two-by-four out of your own eye and then you will be able to see well enough to help that brother or sister with that speck in her or his eye." In other words, take care of your big problem and then you can help your brother or sister deal with their little problem.

Sometimes there are little problems that look like a big problem because our eyesight is all messed up. That two-by-four just keeps on getting in the way. So God says quit hovering around somebody else's address. Quit peeking in somebody else's window. Stop looking in somebody else's mail. Quit being so preoccupied primarily with somebody else's house. Go home and start at your house!

Include God's House

Once we start at our house, we should then go to God's house, the local place of worship. If the church of Jesus Christ is ever going to effectively help the community, the unsaved, the desperate, the damned, and address the negative, self destructive, pessimistic oppressive people and powers that be, then there are some idols in the house of God that we are going to have to address.

There are some little 'g' gods that we are putting before God in the house of God. Sometimes when we come to church, we are not worshiping God, but we are worshiping our ability to worship God. Sometimes I wonder if at times we have become such specialists in worship that our worship stops being about God and becomes all about how well we think we worship God. That idol has to go.

Or perhaps it's not God who we worship but our positions, ministries and agendas. And God can't get in the plan because we are too busy worshipping the plan - you know, our own way of doing things. God wants to do a new thing, but God can't because we are too busy tenaciously clinging to our own thing for our own benefit. If we are going to be the church of Jesus Christ then there are some idols we have got to tear down.

Money is one of the idols, which is why some members won't tithe. Or perhaps money has become such an idol to the church that some churches not only lower their standards to fill the pews but pastors edit their sermons to fill the coffers. God says, "Tear it down."

Power may be one of our idols. That's why some members won't move over, share power and let somebody else help. God says, "Tear it down."

Some pastors have become idols. There is nothing wrong with a healthy respect for godly leadership and positions of authority. We ought to give credit where credit is due. In fact, the Bible says that faithful pastors are worthy of double honor. But instead of some pastors pointing the people to God, they are focusing all of the attention on themselves. God says, "Tear it down."

Fear is one of our idols. That's why we won't step out on faith. In the beginning of the ministry, God blessed the ministry because you were willing to take Holy Spirit inspired risks for the sake of the Kingdom. But now that you have a little money saved up and a few extra ministry buildings and some new ministry trinkets you won't take any more risks because you are afraid of losing the new stuff you have. God says, "Tear it down."

Tradition is one of our idols. Traditions have their place. And good traditions ought to be celebrated, appreciated and preserved. But when tradition gets in the way of the work, will and way of God and becomes more important than people, it becomes an idol. We can't use 1950s methods to address present day issues just because of tradition. God says, "Tear it down."

Comfort and security are idols for some churches. There are some things that God is urging us to attempt, to risk, to try, but we won't do it because it makes us uncomfortable. So we won't take the risk and launch out into the deep. But you can't accomplish anything great hugging the safety of the shallow water. If you want to catch big fish you have to get out in water over your head! We cannot become so addicted to comfort and security that we make an idol out of them and end up ignoring the voice of God. God says, "Tear it down."

Some have made an idol of popularity and prestige. There are some churches that have become too impressed with people in the world because they have power and notoriety. We are too impressed with celebrities, politicians, wealthy business persons, rich athletes and a host of others. As a consequence, we become star struck, treat them like rock stars and in an effort to be associated with them, we create unholy alliances, become unnatural bed fellows and forfeit the call to speak truth to power. We ought to show respect for public officials and leaders in business and community institutions, to be sure. And where we can work together for the common good and kingdom outcomes, we do well to forge healthy relationships. But the church of Jesus Christ belongs to Christ! And there is a difference between forging friendships and having illicit intercourse. We cannot be so impressed with people in power that we make idols out of them and stop holding them accountable. God says, "Tear it down."

In order for the church to be a deliverer, sometimes Christians have got to be delivered. In order for the church to make a difference in the community we have got to let

God be God in God's own house! There are some idols and altars in the church we have got to tear down!

Don't Let Fear Stop You

Notice that when Gideon got ready to do what God said to do, Gideon was afraid. And because he was afraid, he decided to tear down the altars *at night*. Now, we may initially criticize Gideon for doing what he did at night. We may surmise that if he had more courage, he would have done it in the day time. But, what I like about Gideon is that he may have been afraid and he may have done it at night, but at least he did it!

You may be afraid. You may, in your heart of hearts, really want to be rid of that idol. But you've become so dependent upon it. You've become used to it. You like having it around. I know it can be painful and personally threatening to part with it. But, please understand that if God is calling you to do it, even if you're afraid, go ahead and do it. Be courageous. Courage isn't simply doing something in the absence of fear, but often real courage is doing something in spite of your fears.

Let's just be honest. One of the reasons why some of us are personally paralyzed right now is because of fear.

God has given you an assignment. God has given you a mission. Perhaps God has called on you to start at your own house. God wants you to get rid of some things at your house, in your family, in your own relationships. But you are frightened of those who you will have to face. But go ahead and do it and remember that God is with you!

The enemy does not want things to get better in your life. And one of the things that he uses to keep things the same is to stir up your fears. The enemy convinces you that it can't be done and you can't do it. He convinces you that God will help others but God won't help you. He wants you to be too afraid to move, but the scriptures teach that "God has not given us the spirit of fear, but of power and of love and of a sound mind." God says, "Tear it down."

That's what you ought to do with all your idols—all the money, all the power, all the fear - everything that has become more important in your life to you than God. After you chop it up, put it on the altar. After you give it up, give it up to God.

Don't you trust God with it? One of the reasons why we won't give it over to God is that we just don't trust God with it. We trust ourselves with it more than we trust God. That's why we won't let go of it and say, "God, do whatever you want to do with it." Or at least give it to God by asking God what God wants us to do with it. We're afraid that somehow God is going to trick us, that God is going to keep something good from us. But those thoughts are doubts that come to us compliments of the enemy and our insecurities. If you can trust God with your eternal soul, can't you trust God with everything else? If you can trust God to give you eternal life "over there," can't you trust God with your everyday life over here? Whatever you chop up and get rid of, put it on the altar and set it on fire. God told Gideon to burn it! Sacrifice it to God! Trust it to the Lord! Trust God with your job choice. Trust God with your spouse choice. If you can trust God to save your soul can't you trust God to choose your soul mate? Trust God with your marriage. Trust God with your finances. God can do more with it than you can. Trust God with your family. Trust God to help you choose your friends. Trust God with your future. Trust God with everything! Don't ever let anything become more important to you than God. Put everything on the altar and offer it to God and watch what God will do with it!

Don't Just Tear Down, Build Up!

But God didn't simply tell Gideon to "tear down." God also told Gideon to "build up." God is not in the business of just tearing down. God always has a purpose when God says tear it down. Tearing down is the prelude to something else. When you get rid of one thing, God wants you to replace it with something else. Get rid of the bad, but replace it with the good. Get rid of the good and replace it with what's better. Get rid of what's better and replace it with the best. Get rid of mediocrity and replace it with excellence. Get rid of fear and replace it with faith. Get rid of excuses and replace it with plans. Get rid of bad habits and replace them with new habits. Get rid of being a mere spectator and replace it with becoming a participant. Get rid of the altars of Baal but build up the altars of God.

You know what we need? We need more people who specialize in building up. We've reached our quota of people who are always tearing down what's good. In fact, they've become excessive in their tearing down and often they are interested in tearing *you* down. We've got enough people who will only tear down. We now need some people who, after it's down, will build something positive in its place.

After all, it's easy to stand around and talk about how bad that torn down place looks. God wants some people to quit complaining, roll up their sleeves and get down to the business of building something up that's worthwhile. And perhaps the reason why some people don't want to build up is because it takes more effort to build up than it does to tear down. But if things are going to get better, we've got some building up to do. We have families to build. We have communities to build. We have faith and hope to build. We have healthy bodies to build and useful knowledge to build. We have loving relationships to build. We have neighborhoods, better schools, and relevant churches to build. We have positive, powerful and liberating institutions and financial endowments to build. We have to build scholarship funds and then build people to use them. We have strategies to build and businesses to build. We have futures to build. We have the kingdom of God to build. We've got a lot of building to do. God didn't just say, "Tear down." God also said to, "Build up."

Doing Right Has Consequences

Gideon did exactly what God told him to do. Gideon did it by night, but he did do it. He tore down the old altars to false gods and he built up new altars to the true God. But once he did it, all of a sudden he had to deal with the consequences of his behavior. And you will discover that when you choose to do the right thing, you may have to contend with controversy. That's important to remember. Just because you are doing right doesn't mean you won't have to deal with wrong. Some Christian teaching these days will give you the impression that if you do right, nothing but right will come your way. But the fact of the matter is, sometimes when you do right, you have to deal with wrong. Sometimes when you do good, you will have to contend with evil. You may be committed to the truth, but that may mean you will have to put up with people's lies. If they crucified Jesus, the best person who ever lived, what makes us think that doing right exempts us from crosses? Gideon did the right thing but he was soon threatened by people who wanted to do him wrong.

The next morning the men of the city got up early. They found their altars torn down and a new one in its place. Isn't that something? The text says that these men got up early in the morning to worship at their altars. They were wrong about what to worship but at least they were committed to doing it! These men were wrong but they were *committed* to what was wrong. The only reason I am bringing this up is because sometimes I wonder if we are as committed to God as we used to be committed to our life before God. When we were living wrong we were totally committed. We committed our time, energy, creativity, finances, brainpower and resourcefulness to doing what was wrong. When it came to our commitment to doing wrong we were like the postal service: neither rain nor sleet nor snow would keep us from our appointment rounds. We would organize, pool our resources, choose our rendezvous points and consistently carry out our wrongdoing with great determination. But when we gave our lives to Christ for some reason some of us didn't bring the same depth of commitment to doing right as we did to doing wrong.

Or maybe our issue is that we are more committed to other things than we are to God and the Kingdom. When it comes to serving God, I can't tell you how many times I've heard people say, *I can't do it because I'm too tired or it's too early or it's too late* or whatever. But by the same token, when the boss calls you in to make that extra money, even if you're tired you'll go. If it's early, you'll go. If it's late, you'll go. All I'm asking is, are we as committed to serving God as we are to serving ourselves?

The men of the city got up early and found out that their altar was gone and a new one was in its place. And they went around asking, "Who did this thing?" And after their investigation, somebody said, "Gideon did it." How about that? People were talking about Gideon and in the process he ended up being accused of doing something good.

Now I know it's hard to believe, but people talk about you. Yes they do. You are a great person and everything, but there are people talking about you. In fact, there is probably somebody talking about you right now. People are just like that. They will talk about you. You can't really stop people from talking about you. But your behavior and lifestyle can help determine what they say when they talk. And, if they're going to accuse you of something, you ought to make sure they accuse you of something good (even if it seems bad to them). If you're going to be guilty of something, you ought to be guilty of doing something good. There ought to be some things that people can say about you that don't make you mad. And if they accuse you of tearing down idols, you ought to say, "Guilty as charged!" When they accuse you of doing right, don't be embarrassed or get mad! You ought to look up to heaven and say, "Hallelujah!" If they're going to talk, give them something good to talk about. Let them say, "Gideon did it!"

Well, they went to Gideon's daddy's house and they said to his father Joash, *"Come out here. We want to talk to your son because your son is getting rid of our idols. Bring him out here so he can die.* And the scriptures say that his daddy stood up for his son.

A Powerful Influence

The first idol Gideon tore down was in his father Joash's house, but look at Joash standing up for his son. I guess when Gideon stood up, it inspired his daddy to stand up. And the truth is that there are some adults right now who have to admit that the good they are doing now did not start with them. It started with their children. Some parents who love the Lord are in church right now because their children started going first. Some of us are in Sunday School now because our children started going first. Some of us are living right because we saw it in our children first.

You know, children have a way of embarrassing you by doing the right thing even when you don't. And they will call you on the carpet about things you told them they ought to do when they see you not doing what you taught them to do. You can't say, "Do as I say, not as I do," anymore. I don't know how they know, but they know better. They know the difference between what you say and what you do, how you talk and the way you walk. And they will embarrass you, not just in your house, but when you get in public by bringing up something inconsistent in your behavior. When that happens, don't look around, putting your hand over your mouth talking about, "I don't know where she got that from." Yes you do! She's been watching you.

Actually when you think about it, much of the positive change that has happened in our country has happened because of the courage of our children. When adults were initially too afraid or just too blind to take steps to initiate change, our children took the initiative. Sometimes we adults end up getting the credit for the change, but often the change was stimulated by our children. Often it was students on college campuses who initiated positive and powerful community, national and global change, movements, marches and causes when adults were too afraid to take the risk. Sometimes when adults kept silent, it was our children who courageously spoke up against bigotry, hatred, racism, injustices and inequities. And often it was their protest, their agitation, their courage and their voice that inspired their parents and other adults to finally stand up and speak out!

Joash stood up because Gideon stood up. Believe it or not, somebody right now is watching you and they would do it if you would do it. They would stand up if you would stand up. They would do right if you would do right. They would tithe if you would. They would come to Church if they saw you coming. They would worship right if you would do it. They would forgive if you would forgive. They would change if they saw you change. They would risk if they saw you taking a risk. They would sacrifice if you would. They would get some help if you would finally get some help. They could come out of the abusive relationship if they saw you do it. They would say something if you would say something. They would read a book if you would. They would go back to college if you would. They would learn a new skill if you would. They would get their GED if you would. They would stop gang banging if you would. They would keep trying if you would. They would start again if you would. They would live sexually pure if you would. They would make better choices if they saw you doing it.

If parents did it, children might do it. If Christians did it, then perhaps non-Christians would consider doing it. If the church did it, maybe the community would do it. I know you don't think you're very important, but someone is patterning their life after you. And they will do it if you would do it. Joash did it because his son Gideon did it!

The men said to Joash regarding his son Gideon, "Bring your son out so he can die..." You know, people will get upset if you mess with their idols. Some will try to kill you if you mess with their idols. If you don't believe me, you scratch their car. You threaten their security. You interrupt their cash flow. You challenge their title and position or talk bad about their prestige. People will kill you over their idols. I don't mean that they'll necessarily get a knife and stab you or get a gun and shoot you in the head. But, they will kill you. They'll kill your reputation. They'll try to murder your motivation. They'll try to commit homicide on your hope. They'll try to kill your joy. They'll try to steal your dreams. They will try to kill you if you mess with their idols.

The Real God

They said "Bring him out here to die." But daddy Joash said in substance, "You leave him alone. Let me tell you why you ought to leave my son alone. You're worried about your idol. Well, the problem is not my son. He is not on trial." Joash was saying that in the rival analysis, if your god was really a god, you wouldn't have to defend him; he'd do it himself!

That's the difference between the real God and an idol god. An idol god can't do anything for you, not for real. Joash was saying that they ought to put their weapons away and let their god stand up for himself because if their god was real then their god could *do* something. The prophet Jeremiah said that the problem with idols is that they have eyes but they can't see. They have hands but they can't provide. They have feet but they can't come to your rescue. They have arms but they can't embrace you. The problem with idols is that they're man-made and when the enemy comes, you've got to pick up your god and run to safety. They can't do you any good. (Jeremiah 10:5) Now, who would serve a god that they have got to pick up in times of trouble? I need a God who can pick me up in times of trouble!

Conclusion

God is real. The God of Abraham, Isaac and Jacob is real. The God who came in Christ is real. And our very real God did something. God came in Christ, lived a perfect life, died a sacrificial death, but got up three days later with all power in his hands. Love made God do it. And God did it so that you and I might be drawn by that love to have a personal relationship with God through Jesus Christ. Whatever stands between you and a personal relationship with Jesus Christ, "tear it down" and receive Christ today. Then build up a place in your heart that belongs to God and begin to experience the abundant life that only the real God can provide.

CHAPTER 3

ENOUGH IS ENOUGH

[33]Then all the Midianites and the Amalekites and the children of the east were gathered together, and went over, and pitched in the valley of Jezreel. [34]But the Spirit of the LORD came upon Gideon, and he blew a trumpet; and Abiezer was gathered after him. [35]And he sent messengers throughout all Manasseh; who also was gathered after him: and he sent messengers unto Asher, and unto Zebulun, and unto Naphtali; and they came up to meet them. [36]And Gideon said unto God, If thou wilt save Israel by mine hand, as thou hast said, [37]Behold, I will put a fleece of wool in the floor; and if the dew be on the fleece only, and it be dry upon all the earth beside, then shall I know that thou wilt save Israel by mine hand, as thou hast said. [38]And it was so: for he rose up early on the morrow, and thrust the fleece together, and wringed the dew out of the fleece, a bowl full of water. [39]And Gideon said unto God, Let not thine anger be hot against me, and I will speak but this once: let me prove, I pray thee, but this once with the fleece; let it now be dry only upon the fleece, and upon all the ground let there be dew. [40]And God did so that night:

for it was dry upon the fleece only, and there was dew on all the ground.

(Judges 6:33-40 KJV)

Simply wanting things to change is not enough to change them. You will be sentenced to the same old things until you take action to change them. And sometimes the motivation for taking action is when you are sick and tired of the way things are. Even Jesus can't help you if you choose to let things remain the same, to settle for the way things are. But God can work with you when you just *can't* take it anymore, when you just *won't* take it anymore, when you have had it up to here and it's the last straw. If you are fed up with being defeated, frustrated, depressed, abused and down then you are in a good place for God to help you. God wants to help you, but sometimes God is just waiting for you to get to the point where you just say "enough is enough."

So far Gideon's campaign has been a success. So far so good. He has responded to God's call to be a deliverer and has faithfully initiated his plan of "de-idolatrizing" the people of God. So, everything seems to be going along well. But then, something happened. Right after this program of getting rid of idols and replacing idol worship with the pure worship of God, something else begins to take place.

Now, it's not anything new, mind you. It was the same old thing that had been happening every year for about seven years. Verse 33 says that the Amalekites and company began to gather in the Valley of Jezreel to do what they had been doing all along. They were gathering to begin their annual assault on the Israelites. They were coming to scatter Israel to the hills; to steal their livestock; to forcibly take from them what the Lord had blessed them with.

The Spirit of the Lord

And so, in the minds of the enemy it was just another harvest time like any other. There was nothing particularly odd, different or special about it in their mind. For them it was business as usual. But little did they know that while *they* may have been the same, Israel was not the same. While things looked the same, they really weren't the same. The Bible says that the enemy gathered to do what they had always done every year for the past seven years, but then verse 34 begins by saying "But the Spirit of the Lord came upon Gideon." That was the turning point. That was the difference. Things were going to change because "the Spirit of the Lord came upon Gideon."

Now, this translation in the King James Version is really a watered down rendering of the original text. The text here says: "But the Spirit of the Lord came upon Gideon." But the original language says something more poignant. The original language says: *but the Spirit of the Lord **put on** Gideon.* It's saying that the Spirit of the Lord put on Gideon like clothes. The Spirit took Gideon and put Gideon on.

Now, I know you're used to hearing it the other way around, but that's what the Hebrew says. The Spirit of the Lord took Gideon and put him on like clothes. It's a metaphor. What it's seeking to communicate is that Gideon looked like Gideon on the outside, but he was full of the Spirit of God on the inside. That means that you've got to be careful messing with people who are full of the Spirit. When you mess with them, they may look like themselves on the outside, but on the inside it's the Spirit of the Lord! That means you are not fighting them; in reality, you are fighting the Lord!

The Bible says that the Spirit of the Lord put on Gideon. Gideon was so full of the Spirit that there was nothing left on the inside of him but God. And you know, that's what God needs more of if there is going to be a difference made in the world. God needs some people who will be so sold out to Him that there is no room in them for anything but God. God will have their hands and feet. God will look through their eyes and speak with their mouth. God will influence their minds and love through their hearts. If only we had more people who had no room on the inside for anything but God, we could turn the world upside down!

The Spirit of the Lord put on Gideon. Gideon was filled up, he was infused, he was endowed with the Spirit of God! Whenever God gets a hold of your life like that, whenever God possesses you like that, whenever God fills you like that, God takes you to heights that you do not dream. God will do things with your life that will surprise you and those who thought they knew you! If only we would let God just have God's way in our inner lives. The Spirit of God put on Gideon and Gideon was not the same as he was before.

Perhaps it is your testimony that the turning point in your life is expressed in this phrase: *but the Spirit of the Lord.* You were lost in sin, disconnected from God—*but the Spirit of the Lord* saved you and now you have a personal relationship with Christ. Maybe you were hooked on cocaine, a junky just like others, *but the Spirit of the Lord* set you free. You were a single parent hooked on handouts and your friends and foes told you that it would always be that way, *but the Spirit of the Lord* gave you power to go to school and learn a skill, power to keep believing through tough times, power to find a job, and now you are a provider for your family. Perhaps you were living in fear, paralyzed by its power— *but the Spirit of the Lord...*Weak, *but the Spirit of the Lord*...Hungry - *but the Spirit of the Lord*...Depressed, *but the Spirit of the Lord.* You were down for the count, ready to give up and give in, *but the Spirit of the Lord.* Painted in a corner, *but the Spirit of the Lord.* Doors shut in your face, *but the Spirit of the Lord.* Hell hounds were at your heels, *but the Spirit of the Lord.* You should still be in the gutter, *but the Spirit of the Lord.* It wasn't you. It wasn't your education. It wasn't your friends. It wasn't your enemies. It wasn't your determination, will power, creativity or ingenuity that ultimately made the difference, but it was *the Spirit of the Lord!*

Please don't underestimate the power of that truth. The Spirit of the Lord made a difference for Gideon and Israel and if there is anyone who is going to make a difference in our lives, in our communities and in our neighborhoods ultimately it will be the Spirit of the Lord. And we who claim to be filled with the Spirit of the Lord need to know that His power will help us reach out to gangs, face intimidating violence, alter self destructive lifestyles and address the problems that plague our communities. *Not by might, nor by power, but by my Spirit saith the Lord* (Zechariah 4:6).

I wonder if you're tired of the same old thing. I wonder if you're weary of always being under the circumstances. I wonder if you're frustrated with the same old bad habit. I wonder if you're sick and tired of being depressed. I wonder if you're tired of being a victim, tired of being defeated; tired of evil having the last word. Well, if there's ever going to be a change in your life, here it is: *but the Spirit of the Lord.* The Spirit of God is prepared to be the influence that literally transforms your life.

The Spirit of God in your life may have been the turning point in your life, and that's where the turning point is in our text. Look at what God has done with Gideon.

God has taken him from hiding at the wine press and put him on the battlefield. God brought him from complaining about his situation to participating in his deliverance. God has brought him from being filled with fear to being full of faith and power because of the Spirit of God!

The text indicates that once Gideon was full of God, he looked at the other side of the valley and saw the enemy, but even though they were the same, he wasn't. He wasn't afraid anymore. Perhaps you can identify with that, too. You know how it was in your past. You remember how the enemy used to intimidate you, victimize you and just have his way. But then you gave your life to Christ and the Holy Spirit filled and influenced you and now you look at the same situation but you are not afraid anymore. It's like saying to the enemy "Alright, you're going to do what you have always done, but I am not going to do what I have always done! Things have changed because I have changed!

A Call to Action!

The text reports that Gideon grabbed the trumpet and he started blowing it. He started blowing the trumpet while he was filled with the Holy Spirit, full of God's anointing. God's leaders need to be anointed. And I'm not simply referring to leaders who are in the pulpits. I'm referring to leaders anywhere. There are some things you've got to be anointed to do. You can't lead God's people if you are not anointed. You may be the president of this auxiliary or you may be giving leadership to some ministry, but your prayer ought to be, "Lord anoint me!" You need to be anointed. I don't mean you need to be educated (though education is important); I mean you need to be anointed. I don't mean you need to have prestige and power, I mean you need to be anointed. I don't mean you need to have social networking skills or be pretty, popular, handsome or even heaven bound. If you're going to lead God's people you need some Holy Spirit anointing. Anointing is *divine enablement*. You need divine enablement. If you're going to lead God's people, you need God's Holy Help, God's divine assistance. You need to be anointed.

Gideon started blowing the trumpet because he was using it to call the troops. Essentially he was saying to the enemy, "No more business as usual. No more status quo. I'm going to gather some soldiers to come against you this time." Here's another word for some anointed leaders.

When you are really anointed and you sound the trumpet, so to speak, those who really belong to the Lord will respond. You don't have to guess who really belongs to the Lord. When you blow the trumpet, when you sound the alarm, when you declare the vision, when you make plain the mission and summon people to answer the call to serve, you will know who is sold out to God. All you have to do is blow the trumpet and God's real people will show up. There are some people who say that they are soldiers but they never show up when the trumpet sounds. They never come when it is time to do battle. They don't mind staying in the barracks. They don't mind being blessed by all of the benefits of being a part of God's army. But when you blow the trumpet, when you sound the alarm, when you call the troops for battle you cannot find *them* anywhere!

This is also a word for anyone who takes on a God-inspired, worthwhile cause. You may start out addressing issues, challenges or causes that affect your family or neighborhood all by yourself at first. But once you blow the trumpet, once you make up your mind to take action and start talking about what ought to be done, God has a way of sending people to help. You might start out alone, but once you start, you will be surprised by how many other people share your concerns. Don't let the fact that you seem alone stop you from taking action. Blow the trumpet and watch God work! People may not come immediately but if you believe God is behind your cause, blow the trumpet, move forward and trust God to bring the troops.

Gideon blew the trumpet and the first person to show up was Abiezer. Now, the name Abiezer refers to a household. Abiezer was of the household of Joash, the father of Gideon. This means that while Gideon's household was the first place where the idol was torn down, his household was also the first to show up for duty. Tearing down the altars at their home was an act of obedience and consecration (to set yourself apart to be used by God). And consecration leads to preparation. And whoever is first to consecration and preparation is ready to report for duty!

Have you ever seen that United States military poster with the figure of Uncle Sam on it pointing at the onlooker with the phrase beneath it saying "Uncle Sam wants you!" Well, the Lord wants you! God wants you to enlist in his effort to bring about a positive, Kingdom of God change in the world. Believer, if you will discard those things that are not pleasing to God from your life and set yourself aside to be used by God—and unbeliever, if you would repent of your sins, trust God with your life and give your life to Christ— then that would be the equivalent of reporting for duty and you will begin to discover the purpose and power the Lord has for your life.

Abiezer showed up first. Then all of the other tribes that they sent messages out to showed up and gathered around Gideon. When Gideon called them together, he drew a line in the dirt, if you will, and said, "It's time to fight now." In a real sense he was saying, "I'm tired of the enemy taking everything God gives us. I'm tired of living in these caves in fear. I'm tired of the enemy taking our livestock. Every time we work hard the enemy comes in and takes what we've worked so hard to have. I've had it! Enough is enough!"

Can you identify? Am I writing to you? Maybe in order for a change to come in your life you need to quit complaining, fussing and cussing and get to the point where enough is enough. God can't do much if you are satisfied with your negative situation. But if you ever get to the place where you're tired of it all and you can't take it anymore, and you've had it up to here, then you are poised, positioned and postured for God to intervene! You ought to thank God when it's the last straw, when you're tired of being down, defeated, victimized and living below your privilege. You ought to thank God when you get to the place where you are sick and tired of business as usual. When things finally get that bad, then maybe God can affect some change in your life and use you to effect some change as well.

Gideon says, "Not this time!" I dare you to say that. Instead of giving up, maybe you need to say "Not this time!" When you finish reading this chapter or completing this book, and make up your mind that things are going to change, understand that the enemy is going to gather like he gathered before to do what he did before, but you need to say, "Not this time!" If you've got holes in your pocket but you want things to change, you need to say, "Not this time!" If you are tired of the enemy messing with your marriage I dare you to say, "Not this time!" If fear has kept you from starting that business or beginning that ministry or writing that book or looking for that job or applying for that promotion or going back to school or risking a new relationship or stepping out on faith or just saying 'yes' to Jesus, you need to say to your fears, "Not this time!" Go ahead, square your shoulders, straighten up your back and say to yourself, with all of the faith you can muster, "Not this time!"

Now remember, Gideon was not just saying this for himself. Gideon was saying this for his people. It was not just an individual conviction, it was a conviction that had corporate consequences. Gideon wasn't just fed up with the way things were going for him. Gideon was fed up with the way things were going for his people. When God starts to work in your life, God wants you to be delivered so that you can help deliver others. God wants to get your life together so that He can use you to help get your family together, or your community together or your state together or this world together. God wants you changed, free, delivered, whole, filled, empowered and transformed so that God can use you to help bring about justice, peace, salvation, deliverance, joy, wholeness, and transformation to the oppressed, marginalized, lost, excluded, mistreated and empty people around you! What God was doing for Gideon was not just for Gideon, but it was through Gideon for the benefit of Israel!

The Sign of the Fleece

Now, Gideon was encouraged by an angel, filled with the Spirit and surrounded by able bodied men preparing for battle, but Gideon still had one last request. Gideon was a bit hesitant because Gideon wanted to make sure that he was right. Gideon wanted to win this war and he wanted to make sure that the message he had received from God was correct. So, he says in substance to God, "Now, if you're really going to give victory in my hand, my hesitation isn't because I don't think *you* are able, it's that I've got a problem with you choosing *me*. I know how messed up I am. I know what my thoughts are. I know what my failures and weaknesses are, so things have gotten a little cloudy and ambiguous because I know how I can be sometimes. So God, if you're really going to give victory by my hand, I need you to confirm it for me. I need you to show me a sign to confirm what I believe you said to me. I need some visible verification that you have indeed chosen somebody like me. This is how I want you to do it. If you don't mind, Lord, this is how I want to verify it. I've got some fleece and I'm going to take the fleece and I'm going to lay it on the threshing floor. I want you to soak the fleece with dew and leave the ground around it dry. If you do that then I'll know for sure that you're going to give victory at my hand."

So, Gideon set the fleece out on the threshing floor - the hard, cold ground - and when he got up the next morning it was just as he had asked. The fleece was soaked with the morning dew but the ground around it was bone dry. Gideon got his answer.

But then it occurred to Gideon that there was not anything necessarily unusual about what had happened with the fleece because fleece has a natural tendency to draw moisture anyway. If you take fleece that has a tendency to draw moisture, put it out in the open air and onto a hard, cold threshing floor that does not attract moisture, then chances are you might get a fleece that's wet and a ground that's dry.

So, Gideon concludes that what has happened might just be natural and not supernatural. So he says: "God I've got one last request. I need you to do something that can't be done in the natural way so I can know that it's indeed you. God, I'm going to put the fleece out there again, but this time I want you to make it wet on the threshing floor and make the fleece bone dry."

He went to bed that night. I suspect that if he was like you and me he must have gotten ready to get into bed and before doing so got down on his knees and said, "Now Lord, remember what I'm asking you. We're getting ready to go into battle and I've got to be sure that you are with me. Without you I'll go nowhere, but with you I'll go anywhere. So, Lord, please grant me my request."

The text says that he got up the next morning and it was just as he had requested. He saw that the ground around the fleece was soaking wet, but the fleece that has the tendency to draw moisture was absolutely dry. And at that moment, Gideon's call was confirmed. He knew for a fact that the Lord was with him. And since he knew that the Lord was with him, he had courage to do what the Lord wanted him to do. Divine confirmation is a powerful thing for those who are motivated by certainty of God's call and approval.

That's one of the things that was important about Jesus' baptism. Do you remember what happened when Jesus was baptized? He had gotten into the baptismal line with sinners even though he knew no sin. But he perceived that God wanted Him to get in line to identify with the plight of the fallen humanity. And when He was baptized and came up out of the water, the heavens rolled back back like a scroll, the Holy Spirit descended on him like a dove and Jesus heard the audible voice of his approving Father declaring "This is my beloved son in whom I'm well pleased." (Matthew 3:17)

That was simply God saying to His Son "I approve of the decision you have made. I approve of the direction you're going in. I approve of the mission you are on. I'm with you." And it's important to have a sense of God's approval because when you get God's approval you get God's backing. If God isn't in it, then God can't support it. But if God is with you, God will put all of heaven at your disposal!

I don't know about you, but that's all I really want to know whenever I try anything for the Kingdom. All I really want to know is, God, do you approve? I don't care who comes against me; I just want to know if God approves. If God approves then it is easier to face the trials and tests that come. Believing that God approves and supports your actions and intentions gives a sense of courage and peace.

Now, there is something about the dew I want to mention. I believe that the dew on the fleece is significant. I believe that there's some message in the dew because

Hosea says that the blessings of God come to Israel like the descending dew. (Hosea 14:5) Dew has powerful symbolic implications. Dew is the symbol of God's approval. It is a symbol of salvation. It is a symbol of Shalom or peace. In a real sense, dew means God's peace. Dew means having everything you need. Dew is *divine* peace. Let me go further. When Elijah asked God to answer him in the presence of the 450 prophets of Baal, God answered by fire. But God doesn't just answer by fire. Sometimes God answers with dew. You see, sometimes what you need isn't fire. Sometimes what you need is dew or peace. Now, sometimes you do need some fire. You do need some inspiration. You do need some burning. You do need some purging. You do need some passion. But, when you step out to do what the Lord commands and the enemy is swirling all around you, and there's chaos everywhere, what you need then isn't just passion, you need peace. You don't need the peace that the world gives, but you need God's kind of peace; a peace that the Bible declares surpasses all understanding.

I'm sure you've had your challenges. I'm sure you've had your share of life's storms. Have you ever been in a storm so fierce and threatening, tossing you like a nautical toy, that it looked like all was lost but in the midst of it all you had a strange kind of peace? God spoke peace to your restless soul. You had peace to keep on going, to keep on believing, to keep on trusting and trying. You had peace to stand still and see the power of the Lord!

Yes, God not only answers by fire, but God also answers by dew. God gives strength and peace. So when you get to the point where you're tired of your personal status quo, you're sick and tired of the way things are, you're tired of Satan getting the last word in your life, when you get to the place where you just can't take it anymore and you say "enough is enough", then you have put yourself in a position to be used by God to be delivered and be used to help deliver others. And when you step out on God's word to challenge what has been getting the best of you, God can and will give you peace. God can give you peace that confirms that you are doing God' will, making the right choices and stepping out with God's power, presence and protection. And when you have had enough of what the enemy has done and you are ready to make a change, sometimes just knowing that God supports what you are doing is enough. That can begin to happen if you

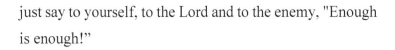

just say to yourself, to the Lord and to the enemy, "Enough is enough!"

CHAPTER 4

STRENGTH THROUGH SUBTRACTION

[1]Then Jerubbaal, who is Gideon, and all the people that were with him, rose up early, and pitched beside the well of Harod: so that the host of the Midianites were on the north side of them, by the hill of Moreh, in the valley. [2]And the LORD said unto Gideon, The people that are with thee are too many for me to give the Midianites into their hands, lest Israel vaunt themselves against me, saying, Mine own hand hath saved me. [3]Now therefore go to, proclaim in the ears of the people, saying, Whosoever is fearful and afraid, let him return and depart early from mount Gilead. And there returned of the people twenty and two thousand; and there remained ten thousand. [4]And the LORD said unto Gideon, The people are yet too many; bring them down unto the water, and I will try them for thee there: and it shall be, that of whom I say unto thee, This shall go with thee, the same shall go with thee; and of whomsoever I say unto thee, This shall not go with thee, the same shall not go. [5]So he brought down the people unto the water: and the LORD said unto Gideon, Every one that lappeth of the water with his tongue, as a dog lappeth, him shalt thou set by himself; likewise every one that boweth

down upon his knees to drink. ⁶And the number of them that lapped, putting their hand to their mouth, were three hundred men: but all the rest of the people bowed down upon their knees to drink water. ⁷And the LORD said unto Gideon, By the three hundred men that lapped will I save you, and deliver the Midianites into thine hand: and let all the other people go every man unto his place.

(Judges 7:1-7 KJV)

A New Lease on Life

Gideon has a new determination. He is fresh from an intoxicating experience with the Holy Spirit and is now surrounded by men whose hearts are still ablaze with enthusiasm after hearing a trumpet blown by Gideon, newly anointed man of God. Both Gideon and the men are facing their enemies with a new purpose and a new power.

Their story opens in chapter seven with Gideon and the men having a new lease on life. It is so fitting that this new chapter starts this new beginning. The people of God were reaching for a new future and striving for a new destiny. They were tired of their past and wanted to claim God's future for their lives.

Have you ever been there? Have you ever been tired of your past? Have you ever been ready for a new future? Well, that's where they were—tired of their past and ready for a new future. Now with a promise from God and confirmation of that promise that came compliments of the sign of the fleece, Gideon was ready to start all over again.

Chapter seven verse one begins with Gideon's new name. It reads "Then Jerubbaal that is Gideon." It starts with Gideon's new name because Gideon is a new man. And often in scripture when God gives a person a new future it is symbolized by God giving them a new name. In the Hebrew culture you didn't just *have* a name, you *were* your name.

Abram had a fresh encounter with God and so God changed his name from Abram to Abraham and his wife Sarai's name was changed to Sarah. (Genesis 17:5,15) Jacob, whose name means trickster, supplanter or heal grabber, had an encounter with God and God changed his name from Jacob to Israel which means "Prince with God." (Genesis 32:28) When Peter met Jesus, Jesus said, "Your name has been Simon but now I'm going to call you Peter." (John 1:42) Peter means rock. Jesus was saying in substance, now you are unstable Simon but when I get finished with you, you are going to be stable, reliable, like a rock. And when Saul met Jesus on the Damascus Road and God changed him, they no longer called him persecuting Saul, but they called him preaching and praying Paul. (Acts 9; Acts 13:9) When you meet God, it's like getting a brand new name because God makes you a brand new person.

Gideon is a new person with a new purpose and a new determination. Jerubbaal means "let Baal defend."That name is a symbol of Gideon's holy indignation, of Gideon standing toe to toe with Baal and saying to Baal, "You claim to be the real God, but I know the real God. You're a fake, Baal, because the God I serve is the one with the power. The God I serve is in a class by himself. Let me prove it to you. I'm going to tear down your altars and let's see what you can do about it!" Jerubbaal—a new name for a new man.

Then the text says in that same verse that after he got this new anointing and had a new purpose as a new person with a new name, that is when it was time to do a new thing. Gideon and the men got up *early* in the morning. I like that. They got up early because they were still excited about what God was doing in their lives. They got up early because they weren't running in fear anymore. They weren't hiding anymore. Their getting up early in the morning was their way of saying to the enemy, "Let's get it on!" They got up early because they were anxious to see if God is true to God's word. They got up early because finally they knew exactly what to do. And, when they discovered what to do, they were anxious to do it.

I wonder what would happen if there were more believers like Gideon who do what they know once they know what to do. There are so many people who know what to do, but they are not doing what they know. You can't get the victory until you do what you know. Truth be told, there are a lot of things that we believers already know to do. We know that we should feed the hungry, clothe the naked and house the homeless. We know that we should visit the prisoner, witness to the lost and forgive our enemies. We know that we should pray for them that despitefully use us, financially support kingdom work and "justly love mercy and walk humbly before our God." (Micah 6:8) There are some things we already know to do, but some of us aren't doing what we know. And God can't bless the way God wants to because of our disobedience.

They got up early! When you find out what God's will is in your life and you really believe His promises and you know that God is no shorter than His word, then you can't wait to do what God has revealed! Whenever you see the light and you know that light is from God, you can't wait to step in God' light! In fact, sometimes you don't get new light in other areas until you begin to walk in the light that you already have!

They got up early and all of them begin to make camp by the well of Harod. Across the valley in the Valley of Jezreel was the enemy—the marauding Midianites and the Amalekites. And, as they looked across the valley they could see one another because they were only separated by a short distance there in the valley. There were 32,000 soldiers ready to fight the enemy. I'm sure that when the Midianites looked at the Israelites they were not intimidated in the least. They had no reason to be intimidated. For seven years they had been having their way with them, so when they look across the valley they were not sweating at all.

But when Gideon and his men look across the valley, what they saw was an incredible sight. Verse 12 says that when they looked across the valley that the enemy's army was like locusts. They were as numerous as grasshoppers and their camels were a numerous as grains of sand on the sea. What an awesome spectacle. If you want to get real specific about the numbers, just look ahead in chapter eight, verse ten and add it all up and it tells you that while Gideon had 32,000 soldiers, the enemy had 135,000. That's a lot of soldiers—135,000 soldiers armed to the tee ready to do battle! But Gideon had only 32,000.

Gideon was outnumbered four to one. But I suspect that Gideon was still encouraged because 32,000 men still ain't nothing to sneeze at, particularly when you have 32,000 men who have a promise from God and who are sick and tired of the way things have been going!

And so I can imagine Gideon with his 32,000 men was encouraged because Gideon no doubt surmised that with a good military strategy even 32,000 soldiers had a chance against the 135,000 they saw across the valley. And I can imagine that Gideon, in a prayerful mood, was talking to God as he strategized. He must have said, "God, now I'm going to need a good strategy. I'm going to need a good plan to handle 135,000 people. I believe I can do it. I've got 32,000 men—32,000 more people than I had when I started. I believe I can do this but you've got to give me the strategy. I believe, God, that through stealth and through preparation and proper planning, and perhaps a strategy of divide and conquer, and maybe a surprise attack at midnight, we can defeat the enemy. So come on God, give me a plan!"

That makes sense don't you think? After all, the same God who called him was the same God who would give him the victory. And the same God who would give him the victory could give him a plan for the victory. It is a blessing to be called of God. But sometimes once God calls us we make the mistake of answering God's call but leaving God in the top drawer at home as we make our own plans. But the same God who called you is the same God you need to consult when it's time to come up with a plan to carry out God's call.

A Strange Strategy

Well, God does indeed give Gideon a plan. But it was a plan that contained the most unusual military strategy that any general had ever heard, especially one who was already outnumbered four to one. God said, "Gideon, the people you have are too many." Excuse me? Can you imagine the amazement in the mind and the terror in the heart of Gideon when, though already outnumbered, God's response is, "You have too many?" What kind of madness is this? What kind of military strategy tells you to reduce the number of soldiers when you're already outnumbered four to one?

Well, as amazing and ridiculous as this may seem, we've got to understand that this text is recorded to remind us of a particular technique that God sometimes employs in order to give us the victory. God was trying to teach both Israel and Gideon how to trust him and not the numbers. God wanted Gideon's confidence to be in God's power and not the power that comes from troop numbers. God was trying to teach them how to ultimately lean and depend on God. Not the numbers but the Lord. Not their power, but His. God wanted them to realize that in order for them to win the battle they must fight with an attitude of complete and utter trust and dependency on God!

Did you know that you can never be too small for God to use but you can be too big for God to use? Have you ever felt within yourself that you don't have what it takes to do what God is calling you to do? Have you ever felt supremely insufficient to carry out the service of the Lord? Have you ever felt too weak to do what you know the Lord is calling you to do? God can use a person who knows and admits their limitations. You're actually in a good position to be used by God because when you know your limitations, you have a tendency to learn how to lean on the Lord.

In fact, you can't have too little for God to use but you can have too much for God to use. For example, the disciples were challenged by Jesus to feed a mass of some 5,000 men, not including the women and the children. (Matthew 14:16; Mark 6:37; Luke 9:13; John 6:5-6) They brought a little boy's lunch with his two fish and five loaves of bread to Jesus and one of his disciples said, "How can we feed them with so little?" But Jesus said in substance, "Give me the food, step back and watch me do the incredible." He took the food, blessed it, broke it and passed it and before He was finished with it, not only was everybody fed but there were 12 baskets left. You can never have too little. Don't disqualify yourself because of what you don't have. Little becomes much when you put it in the Master's hands.

But while you can't have too little for God to use, you can have too much. For instance, God can't fill someone who's already full of themselves. God has a problem using people who are too impressed with themselves. It's difficult for God to use folks who spend a lot of time congratulating themselves, breaking their arms to pat themselves on the back for being so great, thinking about how lucky God must be to use somebody like them with all the gifts they have. When you are like that you're in for a rude awakening and a bitter disappointment because the Bible says that God "resists the proud but gives grace to the humble." If you want to go up, you've got to go down. If you want to be full, you've got to be empty. If you want help you've got to realize that you need help. If you want God to use you, you've got to learn to lean on God. Too much of you may mean too little of God.

In fact, there are some people who let too much money get in the way of trusting God. They trust their cash flow rather than the one who blesses them with cash flow. Some people let too much education get in the way of their trusting God. They depend on their PhD more than they do G-O-D. Some people let too much business get in between them and God. They have 48 hours worth of things they are trying to do in a 24 hour period and so they never have time for God. Sometimes "too much" of something can get in the way of you and God and what God wants to accomplish with and in your life.

Now, when God spoke of Gideon having "too many men" God was not primarily focusing on numbers. God can use 32 or 32,000 to get the victory. God can use small numbers or God can use great numbers. God is not confined to numbers. God has a different enlistment program than we do. We often get hung up on the numbers alone. But God was not concerned about the *quantity* of the soldiers. God was concerned with the *quality* of the soldier. God was not as concerned about how many soldiers filled the heart of the valley as he was concerned about how much commitment filled the hearts of the soldiers. So when God said to Gideon that there were too many soldiers, God meant too many of *the wrong kind of soldiers.*

In a real sense, God was saying to Gideon, "Gideon, things are not the way they appear. You've got 32,000 men, but I want to shake things up a little bit. I want to show you what you're really working with when it comes to your soldiers. It's not their numbers that matter, but it's their character that matters. What I want to do is to weed out who you don't need so you can keep who you do need. And I will do the weeding out with a series of tests."

Test Time

Tests are important. Tests are important because tests have a way of revealing who you really are. Tests have a way of showing what a person is really made of. Tests have a way of putting the squeeze on you and when you are being squeezed whatever is really in you is going to come out.

God has Gideon initiate a series of tests to put the squeeze on his 32,000, if you will. The tests are designed to weed out the bad from the good, the useful from the useless, the artificial from the real, the committed from the uncommitted. The first test God used was the fearlessness test. It was a test based on Deuteronomy 20:8. God says to Gideon "In order for me to show you which of your soldiers are truly dependable, I want you to go to those 32,000 men and announce to them that all who are afraid can pack their bags and go home." God said "Go make that announcement now. I know you think you've got a great army in number but just go make that announcement. I want to show you something."

So Gideon did what God said. Gideon said to the men, "All of you who are afraid, God says you can go home." And the text says that out of the 32,000 soldiers Gideon had, 22,000 soldiers packed their bags, dropped their heads, tucked their tails and went to their home.

Well, when Gideon saw 22,000 soldiers leave he learned a very important lesson. Gideon learned that everybody that shows up is not necessarily with you. Gideon learned that what you see is not necessarily what you get. Gideon learned, in contemporary terms, that the church is always smaller than the crowd. Gideon learned that every soldier that shows up for duty with a uniform on is not necessarily a *fighting* soldier. The tough reality is that some soldiers who put the uniform on are not fighting soldiers they are *parade* soldiers. A parade soldier shows up on special occasions. A parade soldier's motivation for showing up is so that he or she can be seen. They put on all their medallions and decorations and show up on special occasions so everybody will see them and be impressed by them. They like parading themselves in front of everyone. Parade soldiers love to show up for special occasions, but you can't get them to show up when the fighting starts. They like to march but they don't like to fight. They like to wear the uniform but they don't like to get it dirty.

The sad tragedy is that there are some believers like these parade soldiers. They have put on the outward trappings of Christianity without the inner commitment of a Christian. There's more to being a Christian than just showing up and being seen. There's more to being a Christian than the outer trappings of what it means. Anyone can put on the outer trappings of what it means to be a Christian, but the true evidence is not what's happening on the outside; what is more important is what God is doing on the inside. When what God is doing on the inside is real, then evidence of it will show on the outside. And the evidence of true Christianity is not just one's willingness to show up and be seen, but ones willingness to serve and sacrifice for the faith. Being a true Christian does not manifest itself in mere outer image but in inner commitment and character. God was warning Gideon not to be fooled by the crowd who was there in body but not in commitment.

Now, why was it necessary for God to divide the fearful from the rest? Well, first let me define what I think God means in this text by the word "fearful." I want to define fearful so that you will not think that you're automatically disqualified simply because you have some fears. After all, Gideon had some fears and God didn't disqualify Gideon. When God told Gideon to tell those who were afraid that they were excused, he was referring to those who were *controlled* by fear. At best all of us are a mixture of both faith and fear. But, what gets us the victory is when our faith dominates us instead of our fears. When faith is the dominate disposition in your life and fear raises its ugly head, faith will cut it off. When fear tries to get up, faith will push it back down. Every now and then our fears will step forward, but if our faith is strong enough, it will push our fears back. Sometimes fear will knock on your heart's door but when faith opens that door nobody will be there because faith and fear can't occupy the same space.

All of us have some fears sometimes. But there is a difference between those who wrestle with fears and those whose lives are controlled by fear to the point that they make decisions based on fear, craft vision limited by fears and decide what they can and cannot do based primarily on their fears.

God said to Gideon, "I can't use people who are controlled by fear. They'll mess things up every time. I can't use people who take their cues from, make decisions on or decide their actions based on fear." So God decides to weed out the fearful because the fearful have a tendency to focus on the wrong thing. They have got to be eliminated because when they go to battle, they will focus on what the foe can do rather than what the Lord can do. They focus on the mountain and not the mountain mover, on what can't be done instead of on what can be done. They will complain about what seems impossible without realizing that with God all things are possible. They are discouraged by the valley and not encouraged by the one who will go with you through the valley. They fixate on the difficulties of the challenge rather than the one who gives courage and power in the midst of the challenge. God can't use people who are preoccupied and paralyzed by fear because they focus on the wrong thing.

Another reason God had to separate the fearful from the rest of the soldiers is because fear is contagious. In Deuteronomy chapter 20:8 God says, "Get rid of the fearful so that their brothers will not become fearful as well." Haven't you ever been in a meeting where the conversation is full of faith and optimism and people bragging about what God can do, but then a few people— it doesn't take many—start saying things like, *"But wait a minute, I just don't see it. We don't have enough of this and that and we've never done that before..."*? They go on and on until before you know it, their fear has infected everybody around them and the conversation shifts and the atmosphere becomes poisoned with unbelief.

God knew that the fear of the fearful folks was contagious, so God had to thin the crowd. God had to trim the troops. God had to cut down the number. God had to get rid of some folks. That, by the way, is why you should not get too upset when people who said they would be with you choose to excuse themselves when the true challenge begins. When people who promised to participate decide not to because they are afraid of the outcome don't get discouraged. Just stay focused. They might be doing you a favor. Their exit might be God preparing you for victory!

Sometimes God gives strength through subtraction. Sometimes God makes a group strong by making the group thin. Sometimes God will make an individual strong by subtracting something from him or her. Sometimes we are weakened by the presence of too much and too many. We get held up, tripped up or bogged down because of too much and too many—too many privileges, too much doubt, too many of the wrong kind of friends, even too many blessings! Some folks can't stand to be blessed. If they get too blessed with too much, like new wine, it will go straight to their heads and they will start thinking more highly of themselves than they ought. Sometimes too much and too many can mess up what God is trying to do in your life. So, in order for God to rescue us from us, God has to subtract from us. God has to give us strength through subtraction. God will give power by purging. God will subtract in order to add. He will subtract a boring job so that he can add a fulfilling job. God will subtract a bad influence so that he can introduce a good influence. Sometimes God will subtract some money so that we will stop trusting in the money and start trusting in the God who blessed us with the money. Sometimes God will even subtract what is good in order to give us what's better or subtract what is better in order to bless us with what's best! God loves us so much that God will take away what you *want* to show you what you *need*. Sometimes divine reduction is the prelude to elevation and supernatural subtraction precedes a glorious victory!

Well, only 10,000 soldiers remained after 22,000 went back home. But God isn't finished yet. God had another test to thin the crowd even further. God's next test was the water test. The way Gideon and his troops were situated, they could see the enemy across the valley from them. In the middle of the valley was a spring. In order for them to go get water, they would have to go drink from the spring in full view of the enemy. In fact, they were so close in proximity that going down to drink made them more susceptible to ambush.

So God wanted Gideon to take the remaining 10,000 men down to the spring. God didn't tell Gideon or his men what the nature of the test would be ahead of time. You see, life's tests rarely come with a warning. It would be nice if we could get a text or an email every time a test was on the way but that's not the way life works. God doesn't usually come and say, "now tomorrow I'm going to test you," because if you knew about some tests ahead of time and the duration of the test you could fake it through the test.

Let me try to illustrate. Many years ago we were looking for some deacons at the church. The church was growing rather rapidly and we needed, among other things, additional deacons to help care for the people. Someone suggested that we just choose anybody to be deacon because we need deacons so badly. I explained to them that we shouldn't just choose anyone to be deacons just because we desperately needed some. The goal should be to choose people who were deacon material, people who fit the biblical qualifications. But then they suggested that we choose some people, tell them the qualifications for being a deacon, and then tell them we would observe or test them for a year to see if we made the correct choice. I responded that the problem with that approach is that they would know that they were being tested for a year. And if they knew they were being tested for a year, they could fake it for a year. They could pretend to be what we said we needed deacons to be. If you know you're being tested you can tape on artificial fruit. You can pretend to be long suffering, kind, patient and so on.

I said that instead of choosing people to be deacons and then telling them that we are going to observe them to see if they were indeed deacon material, we were going to prayerfully watch people over time without them being aware of it and see how they act when they think no one is watching them. I wanted to see how they passed the test when they didn't know they were being tested. And if they reflected the character qualities outlined in the scriptures without knowing they were being watched then we would know it was for real and not for show and invite them to be deacons. We didn't want to choose people and *make* them deacon, we wanted to watch people and choose those who were already acting like deacons.

That is what God intended when he told Gideon to take the 10,000 men down to the spring to drink. He would test them but not tell them they were being tested. He just wanted them to be themselves. And the way he would test them would be by watching the way they drank at the spring. The way they drank would be insight into the kind of person and therefore the kind of soldier they would be.

Gideon agreed. God had been good to him so far. Gideon trusted him. Gideon took the 10,000 men down to the river. All of them were thirsty and all of them wanted a drink. There was nothing wrong with thirsty soldiers wanting a drink from the spring. If you're a soldier, you need some water every now and then. You have legitimate needs that need to be met. So they went down to the river to drink and soon those 10,000 men fell into two categories by *the way* they drank. The way they drank revealed that they were either 'kneelers' or 'lappers.' Once they arrived at the spring and began to drink, 7,700 of the men, as soon as they saw the water, dropped on all fours, plastered their faces to the water and began to drink without restraint and without really being conscious of what was going on around them. These were the 'kneelers.' God said to Gideon, "Get rid of those." He said "I can't use folks who drink like that. These soldiers are so focused on the water that they forgot about the mission." Their problem was not the fact that they drank water, but the way they drank the water reveals something about their attitude. They were so focused on quenching their thirst that they forgot about the enemy. They were too preoccupied with getting a drink. God told Gideon to get rid of them.

There are basically two reasons why the way those soldiers drank disqualified them from being God's choice for this mission. First, they were so preoccupied with satisfying their thirst that when it was time to drink they drank on all fours. That's dangerous. When you're on all fours, face plastered to the water, you can't see the enemy. If you're a soldier in wartime, with the enemy close by, you keep your eye on the enemy! Jesus said "Watch and pray." (Matthew 26:41) Sometimes you have got to pray with your eyes open! Those soldiers who were on all fours dropped their heads, which lowered their vision. Thirst made them change their disposition about the mission. It was not their top priority anymore. God couldn't use them because they were the kind of men who were ruled by their appetites. And people who are ruled by their appetites will let that undermine their faithfulness.

The second reason they were disqualified was that when they dropped on all fours they also dropped their weapons! And in war time, in plain view of the enemy, you can't afford to put your weapon down. You have got to keep possession of your weapon. Remember, drinking at the water put them in a position for possible ambush by the enemy. And if the enemy attacked by surprise, they can't fight the enemy without their weapons.

Well, Gideon had 300 other men who drank, too, but they drank differently. The Bible says that while the others fell on all fours, those 300 who were just as thirsty as the rest, drinking from the same stream as the rest, did not fall down when it was time to drink; they just knelt down cautiously. They were thirsty and they intended to drink, but they kept their eye on the enemy. They didn't get down on both knees, they just stooped down on one knee. They didn't plaster their face on the water; instead they kept their heads up and used one of their hands to drink like a dog uses his tongue. They took that hand, scooped up water and put it in their mouths. They didn't fall down on all fours because they didn't want to take their eyes off the enemy. And they used one hand to throw water in their mouths because they had to keep the other hand on their weapon.

When you are fighting the enemy for the sake of the kingdom you ought to make sure you keep your eyes on the enemy and keep you hand on your weapon. I know there are some necessary things in life that we have to do, but we'd better remain alert and armed while we are doing them. There are some things that we can enjoy in life that are designed to refresh us, but we should be sure to remain alert and armed. There are some things in life that you've just got to do. You've got to go to work. You've got to go to school. You've got to take care of your children. Every now and then you need to go out on a date with someone. You need to take a vacation. You need to take time to relax, have fun and enjoy life. But you'd better keep your eyes on the enemy, and you'd better keep your sword in your hand. When you go to work, you'd better have your weapon. Standing at the bus stop, you'd better have your weapon. When you are taking care of your children, keep your weapon in your hand. If you're going on vacation, take your weapon with you. Enjoy your life, but keep your weapon in your hand and remember that the enemy is playing for keeps!

Aren't you glad that you've got a weapon? What is our weapon? The sword of the Spirit, which is the Word of God! And every now and then when you're at your workplace and people are putting you through hell, take our your weapon and "Bless them that curse you. Do good to them that hate you. Pray for them that despitefully use you." (Matthew 5:44) When the bill collector knocks on your door, don't you run and hide. Take out your sword and fight your fears by remembering that "My God shall supply all of your needs according to His riches in glory!" (Philippians 4:19) If the doctor shakes his head because he says you're too sick to heal, don't you throw in the towel. Take out your sword and remember that God is Jehovah Rapha; God is still a healer. (Exodus 15:26) If there's no food in the cupboard, don't you go back to selling drugs to make ends meet or selling your body to put food on the table. Take out your sword and remind yourself to be "careful for nothing; but in every thing by prayer and supplication with thanksgiving let your requests be made known unto God. And the peace of God, which passeth all understanding, shall keep your hearts and minds through

Christ Jesus. (Philippians 4:6, 7 KJV)   Take out your sword and fight the enemy!

Conclusion

God is looking for fervent, committed, whole hearted, sold out believers who are jealous for the cause of the Kingdom and who are prepared to make the work of the Kingdom the top priority in their everyday lives. Do you have that kind of commitment to Christ? Do you have the commitment of the 300? If you will make that kind of commitment today, you will see God use you and people with commitment like yours to do incredible and miraculous things. If you don't believe me, keep reading and see how God uses a mere 300 committed soldiers to do the impossible!

CHAPTER 5

JOY IN THE ENEMY'S CAMP

[9]And it came to pass the same night, that the LORD said unto him, Arise, get thee down unto the host; for I have delivered it into thine hand. [10]But if thou fear to go down, go thou with Phurah thy servant down to the host: [11]And thou shalt hear what they say; and afterward shall thine hands be strengthened to go down unto the host. Then went he down with Phurah his servant unto the outside of the armed men that were in the host. [12]And the Midianites and the Amalekites and all the children of the east lay along in the valley like grasshoppers for multitude; and their camels were without number, as the sand by the sea side for multitude. [13]And when Gideon was come, behold, there was a man that told a dream unto his fellow, and said, Behold, I dreamed a dream, and, lo, a cake of barley bread tumbled into the host of Midian, and came unto a tent, and smote it that it fell, and overturned it, that the tent lay along. [14]And his fellow answered and said, This is nothing else save the sword of Gideon the son of Joash, a man of Israel: for into his hand hath God delivered Midian, and all the host. [15]And it was so, when Gideon heard the telling of the dream, and the interpretation thereof, that he worshipped,

and returned into the host of Israel, and said, Arise; for the LORD hath delivered into your hand the host of Midian.

(Judges 7:9-15 KJV)

At the time of this text Gideon has been left with dramatic troop reduction, compliments of the Lord. He started with 32,000 soldiers against 135,000 enemy soldiers. But God stepped in and had the audacity to tell Gideon that he had too many soldiers. He was already outnumbered four to one, but God said, "You have too many." After a series of tests that reduced Gideon's troops to a mere 300 men, God said to Gideon, "Now, you're ready to fight." And, the text reports that the very same night that the troops were reduced, God said, "Now go down to the enemy's camp and take the enemy."

Reoccurring Fears

Now, you can imagine after having 32,000 soldiers reduced to 300 that Gideon was a bit apprehensive. You can imagine that he had to fight with his fears and struggle with some reoccurring doubts. It's one thing to have 32,000 and be outnumbered, but it's another thing to have 300 and be outnumbered.

So you can understand why Gideon would be a little afraid. I mean, I know that God had done some miraculous things in Gideon's past and had reaffirmed His promise that the victory was his. And yet in spite of what God had already shown him and in spite of what Gideon had already experienced, when Gideon is faced with this new challenge, he begins to doubt again. But let's not be too hard on Gideon because often the same is true with you and me. We know that God has done some miraculous things in our past and we know it was nobody but the Lord who did it.

In fact, you may be fresh from some miracles right now. And yet in spite of all that God has done in your past, in spite of all the miracles that God has shown you, in spite of all of the tight spots that God has gotten you out of, in spite of the fact that you know that if it hadn't been for the Lord, you wouldn't be where you are right now, oftentimes when faced with a fresh challenge, we get amnesia and forget what God has already done. And even though God has promised us that He is faithful and has shown us that He will come through for us, sometimes our fears come up against our faith and we struggle all over again.

Well, in a real sense, that's what happened to Gideon. God had promised Gideon victory but now his troops were reduced to 300 and he began to struggle with his fears again. God said "Go down at once now and take the enemy." But he struggled with his fears. The reason why I know that he struggled with his fears is because after God told him to go and take the enemy he said "...*but if you are fearful.*" God knew he was fearful. Then God says, in substance, to him, "I'll tell you what I will do for you. Go down on a reconnaissance mission. If you're afraid to go alone, take your servant with you. Go down to the enemy's camp and when you get there at the edge of the camp, I'm going to cause you to hear something that's going to strengthen your heart. (7:10-11a)

Man, I love God! Let me explain why. The first time Gideon's heart was faltering Gideon *asked* God for a sign. But this time when Gideon's heart is faltering, Gideon didn't have to ask God for a sign; God *volunteered* one. Sometimes you don't have to ask God for encouragement; God will just volunteer to encourage your heart. And the reason why I believe God volunteered to encourage Gideon's heart is because Gideon had become the kind of person who went on in spite of his fears. Even though he had trouble believing, even though he struggled with his doubts, he was willing to obey God anyhow. And God honored his heart with a sign designed to encourage him. Now I understand what the old folk in the church where I grew up meant when they'd say, "If you take one step, God will take two." Sometimes if you will just go in spite of your fears, in spite of your faltering faith, in spite of the fact that it looks like it can't be done, God will volunteer to find a way to encourage your heart!

Lessons from the Enemy's Camp

Gideon was fearful but God said go down and I will drop a word of encouragement on you. So Gideon took God at His word. He and his servant went down that night. It was about the middle watch of the night, somewhere between 10:00 pm and 2:00 am. Gideon went down into the enemy's camp. Can't you see him crouching down like a good soldier? He's a young man and so he's quick and agile. He and his servant slip swiftly yet surreptitiously through the underbrush making sure that they don't tip off the enemy by disturbing some camels tied up nearby. Soon they stop near a guard station or perhaps the tent of the enemy. While there the text says that they hear the enemy talking so they eavesdrop on the conversation. It is dark, they're outnumbered, their hearts are thumping and adrenaline is flowing but they are listening attentively to the enemy talk.

One of the soldiers is saying to his friend, "You know I had a dream." The other soldiers says, "Oh yeah?" He says, "Yeah. I saw a loaf of barley bread and it was tumbling down the hill into our camp and as it tumbled into the camp it hit the tent of the Midianite prince and crushed it. I've been having this dream over and over again and for the life of me I just don't understand it." His friend said, "Uh oh. I know what that means. That's nothing but the sword of Gideon. That's a sign that God has given the son of Joash the victory."

Victory is Already Yours!

Gideon learns several lessons when he overhears the conversation of his enemy. First of all, he learns that the people who he was afraid of were more afraid of him! And my brother or sister, it is important to remember that as you face the powers of evil on behalf of the Kingdom of God, while you are facing the challenges of your life and community, understand that the enemy knows that he is defeated. The enemy knows what we sometimes forget—the victory is already ours! Haven't you heard? It happened about 2,000 years ago. Don't you remember when Jesus was hung up on a cross at Calvary's hill? Don't you remember that he got up from the grave with all power in his hand? He has already defeated the enemy. He has already taken the sting out of death, robbed the victory from the grave, snatched the crown from Satan's head, taken the keys of death, hell and the grave from Satan's waist. God has already called the enemy to court, had his trial, declared him guilty and passed sentence on him! The only thing left is his ultimate execution. But Satan knows that he is already defeated.

That's good news! The only thing left for us to do is fight the good fight of faith. So it doesn't matter how outnumbered we may look. It doesn't matter how lopsided the odds seem. It doesn't matter how many you have on your side. What matters is Who is on your side. Even if it is just you and God, God plus one is always a majority. If God be for us, who can be against us?

Notice if you will that the soldier who shared the dream said that there was a loaf of barley bread that came tumbling down the hill and crushed the tent of the prince of the Midianites. He did not say that it was a loaf of *wheat* bread but *barley* bread. That's important because back then, poor folks couldn't afford wheat bread so they ate barley bread instead. So, in a real sense, barley bread in the dream symbolized the poor, the insignificant, the "nobodies."

What a word! You see, when God called Israel to be his people they were considered by many to be a nation of nobodies. They were not chosen by God because there was something particularly special about them. When God showed up in Egypt while they were in slavery and brought them out, in the eyes of many they were just a hodgepodge of insignificant human refuse. They were nobodies when God delivered them. In fact, they didn't even have any real laws to govern them as a nation. They didn't get the Ten Commandments until they got to Mount Sinai, so they weren't really a nation when God rescued them. But when God got finished with them, they were different than they were when God delivered them.

Early in Gideon's story Gideon felt just like a nobody. When God showed up and called him, Gideon described himself as the least of the least. He said that he was the least person, in the least family, in the least tribe, in a nation of nobodies. But in the enemies dream, that loaf of barley bread, that symbol of nobodies, that symbol of Gideon and the Hebrews, tumbled into the camp of the marauding Midianites and crush the tent of the prince. In that dream, those nobodies got the victory.

Let me share a word to the nobodies for just a moment, all those whom society has left out and looked over, those whom others have convinced are nothing and will never amount to anything. If you are considered by others (and even by yourself) to be a nobody, I've got some good news: Even nobodies can get the victory! In fact, God specializes in using the so called nobodies to do extraordinary things. It is true. All those people whom society deems nobodies—ex-cons, drug feigns, the homeless, no-GED-having, school dropouts, no-brand name-wearing nobodies, people who don't have a title—I'm referring to you. If you've been kicked to the curb, I'm referring to you. If your family and friends have given up on you, I'm referring to you.

Your life matters to God and you can win when you hook up with a holy God. You may have to struggle sometimes. You may have to fall and get back up sometimes. Your heart may falter and your faith may wane, but if you stay hooked up to God, God can give nobodies victory! The good news for the nobodies is that you may have to tumble while you're doing it, like the barley bread in the enemy's dream, but God will cause you to tumble over the schemes of the enemy right into glorious victory.

Gideon overheard what the enemy was saying. God planned to strengthen Gideon's heart, but God didn't send him to a preacher's house. God didn't send him to talk to Missionary So and So. Now, God can and does do that. But this time God chooses to encourage Gideon's heart with a word that comes from the lips of the enemy. God uses the enemy to give Gideon strength.

Did you know that God can even use the enemy to give you what you need to win? I don't care what negative circumstances are that you find yourself in. God can use the negativity of that circumstance to encourage your heart. That is one of the things that makes the power of God so special. God is not just omnipotent; in a real sense God is omni-creative. Some have said that God can use the devil's oven to bake his bread. In other words, God can use what the enemy is doing to carry out His will. Joseph, one of the sons of Jacob, knew this. Once he had become prince of Egypt he looked back over his life and considered all of the cruel things that his jealous and insecure brothers had done to him. And even though he had every reason to let the negative things that they had done to him make him bitter instead he let them make him better. And one of the reasons he was able to look back without bitterness and hate is because despite his brothers' cruelty, indeed because of their cruelty, God brought out His good. God had used their mistreatment to strengthen him on the inside and orchestrate his life so that he could be a blessing to his family and his nation. This realization inspired Joseph to say to his brothers "As for you, you meant evil against me, but God meant it for good in order to bring about this present result, to preserve many people alive." (Genesis 50:20 NASB)

The old folks in the church where I pastor say that "God can hit a straight lick with a crooked stick." The Bible declares, "And we know that all things work together for good to them that love God, to them who are the called according to his purpose." (Romans 8:28 KJV) What happened to Jesus on Calvary was hard, harsh and brutal. But God used what the enemy did to the savior and purchased our salvation. They meant it for evil but God used it for good. Gideon's encouragement came from the lips of the enemy.

The text says that once Gideon heard the enemy confess that victory was his, and he was reminded of what

God had promised in the first place. As soon as Gideon heard the testimony of his victory through the lips of his enemy, he immediately fell down and worshipped God in a spirit of thanksgiving. Gideon is a good role model. Gideon heard the good news of the goodness of God and what God was going to do and started thanking God right then and there. He didn't say 'I can't wait to get back to church to praise God for what I just heard." Gideon understood that praise is portable. You can take it wherever you go. You can do it wherever you are. You don't have to be in church to praise Him. Gideon dropped on his knees and in a spirit of thanksgiving he said "Thank you!"

You don't need stained glass windows to say thank you to God. You can praise him in the break room at your job. You can praise him in the hospital while you're hooked up to IV's. You can give him glory in the car while you drive. When God has been good to you, you can thank God where ever you are. Yes, Gideon rejoiced in the Lord. And he did it in a most unusual place. He worshipped God in the enemy's camp. He was surrounded by the enemy. He was outnumbered by the enemy. There was darkness all around because it was midnight. His circumstances didn't look like a precursor to praise. But in the midst of being outnumbered, overwhelmed and surrounded by darkness, you find a man on his knees praising the Lord!

Can you do that? Can you praise God even in adverse circumstances? You don't have to wait until the sun comes out to praise God. You don't have to wait until you win the victory to shout hallelujah. In fact, Gideon praised God before the battle was even fought. He praised God on the strength of God's promise! You can praise God on the strength of what God promised because God's word is good. The Bible says about God that he is not a man that he should lie. So don't wait until the battle is over to shout! Even in adverse circumstances, even when you're outnumbered and there's darkness all around you, praise God based on what he promised. In fact, God will do what he did for Gideon. In the darkness of your situation he will send his word, even on the lips of the enemy, to give you the grace to hold on! Then like he did for Gideon, God will leave you with joy, even in the enemy's camp. That means though you are sick, you can still have joy. Though you're unemployed you can still have joy. Bills are due and you don't have the money but you can still have joy. Still single and want to be married, you can still have joy. Right in the midst of the enemy's camp—right in the middle of negative circumstances—God can give you joy. God can give you joy by giving you a divine word. Sometimes all you need to make it through the darkness of dark times is a word from the Lord—a word of hope, a word of encouragement, a reminder of His promises, a word that stirs up in you a deep conviction that victory is on the way!

Conclusion

Once Gideon finished rejoicing he ran out of the enemy's camp, back to his own camp and told his soldiers, the ones who were outnumbered, "I just got a word from the Lord. Arise; the victory is ours!" And I have penned these words to report to you, the reader, that I have a word from the Lord for you, a word for all the fainthearted and afraid: Arise! Get up! It doesn't matter what's got you down. Arise! Get up! I don't care how long you've been down. Arise! Get up! No matter how many are against you. Arise! Get up! In spite of the pain, fear, failure or disappointment. Arise! Get up, because, child of God, victory is already yours! Get up! Hold your head up, hold your back straight, square your shoulders, grab hold of your hope, encourage yourself. Things may look bad right now, but God is able to turn things around. And God can start by giving you a word that brings you joy in the enemy's camp!

CHAPTER 6

A TRUMPET, A VESSEL, A LIGHT
AND A SHOUT!

[15]And it was so, when Gideon heard the telling of the dream, and the interpretation thereof, that he worshipped, and returned into the host of Israel, and said, Arise; for the LORD hath delivered into your hand the host of Midian. [16]And he divided the three hundred men into three companies, and he put a trumpet in every man's hand, with empty pitchers, and lamps within the pitchers. [17]And he said unto them, Look on me, and do likewise: and, behold, when I come to the outside of the camp, it shall be that, as I do, so shall ye do. [18]When I blow with a trumpet, I and all that are with me, then blow ye the trumpets also on every side of all the camp, and say, The sword of the LORD, and of Gideon. [19]So Gideon, and the hundred men that were with him, came unto the outside of the camp in the beginning of the middle watch; and they had but newly set the watch: and they blew the trumpets, and brake the pitchers that were in their hands. [20]And the three companies blew the trumpets, and brake the pitchers, and held the lamps in their left hands, and the trumpets in their right hands to blow withal: and they cried, The sword of the

LORD, and of Gideon. [21] And they stood every man in his place round about the camp; and all the host ran, and cried, and fled.

(Judges 7:15-21 KJV)

Equipped with a divine assignment, a promise of victory from God and an affirmation of that promise from the lips of the enemy, Gideon runs from the enemy's camp back to his own camp and arouses his men declaring, "Arise for the Lord has given us victory over Midian." Gideon was excited and anxious to engage the enemy. His attitude has been altered from one of fear to faith and he is now confident that victory is certain. As he encourages his 300 men, they are still grossly outnumbered, but Gideon is learning that what determines the victory is not always how many you have but whose side you're on. And Gideon and his men are on the Lord's side.

After arousing his men for battle Gideon begins to initiate his God-inspired strategy. He took his three hundred men and divided them into three groups of one hundred. Then he gave instructions and some weapons for the warfare. The weapons he gave them were odd weapons indeed. They are unconventional in nature to say the least. He does not give his soldiers swords or shields. He doesn't give them bows, arrows and spears. But as he prepares them for battle he gives each of them a trumpet, a vessel and a light. Now this clearly does not make sense. But God's thoughts are not our thoughts and his ways are not our ways. (Isaiah 55:8) God has this holy habit of resorting to unconventional ways to do his business and bidding. He used a staff in the hand of liberator Moses to split a Red Sea. (Exodus 14:16, 21) He fed Israel in the desert by causing bread to fall from heaven and light to the ground with the morning dew. (Exodus 16) When they got thirsty he caused wet water to come from dry rocks. (Exodus 17) He told a leper named Naaman to wash in dirty water in order to be made clean. (2 Kings 5:10) He told Joshua and the children of Israel to defeat the city of Jericho by merely marching around the city walls and the walls came tumbling down. (Joshua 6:12-20) God used a little boy'lunch of two fish and five loaves to set a banquet table in a desert place to fed 5000 men, not including the women and the children. (Matthew 14:15-21; Mark 6:34-44; Luke 9:12-17; John 6:5-13) And who would have ever guessed that when God got ready to save humanity he would come in the person of Jesus, a poor peasant carpenter crucified on a criminal's cross and resurrected on Sunday morning! Yes, God has some unconventional ways of doing the incredible.

The Best Defense is a Good Offense

Now before I get to the unusual use of the unusual weapons of warfare in our text, there are a couple of principles in the passage that I want to make plain so that they can be a part of your personal practice. First notice that Gideon led his men down to the enemy's camp in order to defeat the enemy. Gideon did not instruct his men to remain in their own camp and wait for the enemy to attack. He didn't tell the men to build a barricade and prepare for the enemy's assault. Gideon led the men down into the enemy's camp to engage them in warfare. That's simply Gideon's way of saying that they were on the offensive.

Whatever else that reveals, it ought to remind every post-resurrection believer that we are not to sit around and wait for the enemy to come to us. Kingdom Christians are not called to be reactive but proactive. Jesus once said to his disciples "Upon this rock I will build my church *and the gates of hell shall not prevail against it.* (Matthew 16:18) That last phrase means that the gates of hell will not be able to withstand the onslaught or attack of God's church. It is a description of the people of God using the power of God to engage the enemy. This means that as the church of Jesus Christ we are not called of God to hide in sanctuaries and build barricades against the evil in our communities. God has not saved us so that we can sit safely within some sanctuary and perpetually sing, "Sweet hour of prayer that has called us from a world of care." God calls us to leave the sanctuary after worship, go down in the enemy's camp and take back territory that doesn't belong to the enemy!

Do you know what territory doesn't belong to the enemy? Those men meandering meaninglessly on the corner without any purpose, they're stolen territory. The crack addict who's hooked on crack, she's stolen territory. The woman who is a single parent who has given up all hope because the enemy has used people to tell her that she has no future, she is stolen territory. That wealthy person who has a full bank account but is spiritually bankrupt, that person is stolen territory. There are scores of people who have been, in one way or another, kidnapped by the enemy and the church of Jesus Christ has been called to take back what the enemy has stolen.

This principle is not only true in the community, but it's also true in our personal lives as well. There is some stuff that Satan has taken from you. But God is saying to you to quit sitting around complaining about what he took! Whatever the enemy has taken God has given you the power to take back what belongs to you. Don't be afraid. The scripture says that "God has not given us a spirit of fear but of power and of love and of a sound mind." I know that it looks like the odds are stacked against you, that you are outnumbered, that you don't have adequate resources, that you don't have what it takes, but be of good courage and dare to believe that you can recover what the enemy has stolen. Go get your peace, go get your joy, go get your family, go get your reputation, *your* self esteem, *your* self worth, *your* self respect, *your* purpose, *your* future, *your* destiny. Don't believe the enemy's lies. Don't settle for what the enemy has determined for your life! Don't play the victim, and don't expect God to do all of the work. Go on the offensive and reclaim what God intended for you.

Leaders as Role Models

So the first thing to remember is that we are on the offensive. The second thing I want you to notice is what Gideon said to the troops as they prepared to go and do battle. In verse 17a he said, "Look on me and do likewise."

And in 17b he says, "As I do, so shall you do." Now, one good key to corporate victory is that you've got to have leadership that is able to say to those whom they lead, "Do as I do." That means that leaders have to be living with a certain level of integrity. One of the questions that some of us who lead in the church need to ask ourselves is, what would become of the ministry that I give leadership to if I were to tell those I lead to do as I do? I wonder what would happen if those who we give leadership to did as we did financially. Would your church ministry have financial abundance or would it be lacking? What would happen if the people we lead did as we do in matters of the heart? Would they forgive or would they use their hearts as a storeroom for old grudges?

The truth is that too many leaders are being one way on Sunday and another way after Sunday. And there are some leaders who display a distinct contradiction in the way they behave in the sanctuary and the way they behave after the benediction. If you are a Christian leader in any way, you ought to be sure to take this to heart! Leaders, if we want to be victorious, we have to be able to say to those to whom we give leadership - "Do as I do." Gideon said to those he was leading, "If you really want to win the victory, watch me!"

In a real sense, this 'do as I do' leadership principle is important in other areas of leadership as well. If you lead in business, or hold leadership in the community, in government, as a parent, in school as teacher or principal, or in some other area in life, leaders earn the most credibility if they lead by example. Leaders ought to be able to say to those whom they lead, "Do as I do."

We need some leaders who have had some victories in their lives so that they can say to those to whom they give leadership, "if you want to know how to win, watch me." Even when you make a mistake, the way you handle your mistake can be a testimony to those who follow you or fall under your influence. When you make a mistake, do you admit your mistake or do you move to the 51st state of the union - the state of denial? Are you too proud to say, "Sorry, I messed up," or "My bad, I was wrong?" When you fail morally, do you go immediately into denial or do you fall on your knees before God and ask God to forgive you of your sins and then move forward trusting in his grace? Even the way we fail is a testimony and example to those who follow us.

There's A Place for You!

The third principle I want you to notice is found in verse 21. It reads "And every man stood in his place roundabout the camp." The third principle is that everyone has a place. One of the keys to victory for the church of Jesus Christ is first of all to know that you've got a place. Amen. That's good news. Everyone in the body of Christ has a place. In the Kingdom of God and in the body of Christ there is no such thing as not being included. The world may say that you don't have a place, but that is not true in the Kingdom of God and that should not be true in the body of Christ.

What is often the problem in the church is that churches are not teaching this principle. Or when they do, they have limited ways for people to serve. They have the same old traditional places to serve like as ushers, deacons, trustees, choir members, clergy, missionaries, and that is basically it. But the church of Jesus Christ must be broader and more creative in her understanding of how and where people can serve so that they can find their place. We still need the traditional places of service, to be sure. But we need to open our minds and help believers to discover new and creative ways to use their gifts, talents, skills and passions for the sake of the Kingdom. We should discover how to teach believers to use their gifts for the sake of the Kingdom in areas like event planning, hospitality, marketing, electronics, media, advertisement, accounting, computers, evangelism, education (both Christian and secular), music and the performing arts, set design, business, nonprofits, mentoring, poetry, painting, drawing, graphic arts, recreation, diet and health, career counseling, college ministries, children's ministries, after school programs, mercy ministries (prison ministry, visitation, clothing, housing, street ministry, etc.), social justice, and a host of other areas of service and Christian influence. If the church would open its mind to these and other areas and teach believers how they may serve the cause of Christ through them, then more believers could find "their place."

Still, while some believers have opportunities, they are still not committed to serving. They are glad they are saved but they behave as if they are saved to sit, satisfied with their salvation, and that's the whole of their Christian life. But believers are called to make disciples and serve. The fact is, too many believers have been praying too long about where they're supposed to serve. They have been members of active congregations for five and six years and still claim that they don't know what the Lord has called them to do. Either they're not seeking and praying or they're just lying. God has called you to do something. You can't be a hero sitting on the sidelines!

In fact, there are some things that all believers are called to do. All of us are called to study God's word. All of us are called to come to worship. "Not forsaking the assembling of ourselves together, as the manner of some is..." (Hebrews 10:25 KJV) All of us are called to give financially to support the kingdom cause. "Bring ye all the tithes into the storehouse..." (Malachi 3:8 KJV) All of us are called to serve others, especially the "least of these." All of us are called to share our faith in order to make disciples of every nation. So there are some things that all of us know we're called to do.

All of us have a place. That truth ought to make your heart glad! Sometimes this world will make you feel like you don't have a place in it, that you don't matter, that you don't have anything to offer, that you don't really belong. But the good thing about the economy of God's Kingdom is that every child of God has a place!

Well, once you find your place, the next thing you ought to do is report for duty. The text says that "Every man *stood* in his place." It is one thing to know where you are suppose to serve, but it is another thing to report for duty. But there are a whole lot of believers who are AWOL (absent without leave). They are not at their post. They are not where they are supposed to be. And we cannot hope to win the victory corporately the way the Lord desires if we have many soldiers out of their place. We have to find our place and *stand* there. That suggests to me that we should not be easily moved. We should not be so quick to quit when things become difficult. When we are working for the Lord and struggling for what is right, righteous and true, then we shouldn't be so quick to throw in the towel at the first sign of trouble. There is too much work to be done and too many people depending on us to do it, for us to be so easily discouraged. The Bible says "After having done all to stand." If we have to struggle, fight and sacrifice then, so be it. And when the dust settles, God ought to be able to find us still standing at our posts. In the black church it is not unusual for the prayers of the saints to be punctuated at the end with the heartfelt words, "Lord, at the end of my journey, I want to hear you say, "Well done." Well, that's a noble desire. But before you can hear, "well done" you have got to "well do!"

"And every man stood in *his* place." Do you know one of the reasons why Satan gets the best of us in the church? It's because we've got too many people standing in somebody else's place. But the text says that "every man stood in *his* place." Another way of saying this is "stay in your lane." In the Olympic Games, in the area of track and field, sprinters can be disqualified for a number of reasons. One of those reasons is if they end up running in another runner's lane. The reason that disqualifies them is that when you run in another runner's lane you can hinder the other runners and even cause serious injuries. I am convinced that one of the reasons Kingdom work gets hampered and folks get hurt is we have too many runners carelessly running all over the place, getting in everyone else's lane.

It's a beautiful thing when every person stands tenaciously and functions faithfully at their posts. The enemy can't handle a church when everybody is at their post. The enemy can't handle a church where everybody is where they're supposed to be cooperating and coagulating in a coordinated and collaborative effort. Everybody can't be a general. Everybody can't drive the tank. Everybody can't be out front. Some people have to be in the back. Some people have to bring up the rear. Somebody's got to serve in the foxhole. Somebody has to be in the mess hall. Everybody must stand in his/her place!

And please consider the following truth: You will never know the real joy and fulfillment of service until you find your place and get in that place and serve in your place. Quit being so jealous of somebody else and the place God has given them to serve. Be faithful in the place and with the task God has assigned to you. We don't get rewarded because of the place where we serve, but based on the faithfulness with which we serve. Every person has a place and every person is important to the body of Christ. And whenever we serve in our place, whenever we do what we're called to do, then we will get the victory and God will get the glory.

I think it's important that I am clear regarding the idea of being "in your place." When I say "in your place" I am not suggesting that your place be based on your gender, race, socioeconomic status or even your educational attainment. Your place in the body of Christ should be determined primarily by your gifts and calling. Furthermore, God does not give gifts based on the aforementioned type of things. And we don't get gifts because we deserve them somehow. In fact, the very definition of *gift* militates against that notion. By definition, gifts are not given because you deserve them. You don't earn gifts; you earn wages. Gifts are given because of love. And God gives us gifts by way of the Holy Spirit based on God's mysterious and incredible love!

God's Winning Strategy

The text reports that once Gideon divided the people into three camps of one hundred, and put everyone in their places, he gave them some odd, unusual, unconventional instructions. Gideon gives each of his soldiers a trumpet, a vessel and a light. And, according to God's instructions they were to use them a particular way. Gideon relayed the following instructions: First, each soldier was given **a trumpet**. The trumpet was a ram's horn and was usually used as an instrument of announcement. When it was blown, it was blown to either announce a celebration or as a declaration of war. In this case, the trumpet would be blown as a declaration of war.

Our mouths are the trumpets that we are to blow in order to trumpet forth the good news of Jesus Christ. Satan wants you to keep quiet about the fact that the kingdom of heaven is at hand. Satan wants you to keep it a secret that Jesus died but didn't stay dead. The enemy wants you to keep quiet about how Jesus got up from the grave with all power in his hand. Satan doesn't want you to tell anybody that if anyone be in Christ they are a new creation. Old things are passed away; behold all things have become new. (2 Corinthians 5:17) The forces of darkness do not want you to trumpet forth God's truth because that's a declaration of war!

But you ought to tell it everywhere you go. The Bible says about the gospel that it is the power of God unto salvation to everyone who believes. (Romans 1:16) The enemy can't handle it when you share the good news.

When Jesus came, he came telling the good news. And when Jesus left, he left his disciples here and he told them to go and tell it. And the command he gave them comes reverberating through the corridors of history reminding every present day follower of Jesus to tell it!

The text says that Gideon gave "every man" a horn. That should remind us that the preacher is not the only person who is supposed to share the gospel of Jesus Christ. Each person gets a horn. Now, it may still be strapped to your waist and you haven't used it lately, but if you've been saved, then you've got a horn. Use it to the glory of God!

In fact, we who are saved today are saved because one day we heard the trumpet ourselves. Somebody blew the trumpet of the gospel of Jesus Christ. Someone shared the good news with us. We heard the trumpet, responded to the call and accepted the savior. He came into our lives and we haven't been the same since! And if the Lord Jesus has really touched us, if he's really changed us, if he's really saved us, if we're really full of his joy, then we can't keep it to ourselves. Take the trumpet off of your waist. Put that trumpet to your lips and tell somebody! Tell them that salvation has come in Jesus Christ. Tell them that he lived, died for our sins, was raised from the dead and is alive forever more. Tell them that Jesus is available to anyone who wants to be saved. Tell them that eternal life is just a prayer away. How can they know if we don't tell them? Gideon gives the men a trumpet. Blow your trumpet if you want to win because the one thing that helps us defeat the enemy is the sword of the spirit which is the word of God.

Notice secondly that Gideon gave them a **vessel** or a clay pot. Now we know what the clay pot can represent for us because Paul says that "we have this treasure in earthen vessels." (2 Corinthians 4:7) That clay pot in the text is symbolic of our lives. Consider if you will that those clay pots in the text were literally used for something else before Gideon got a hold of them. Believe it or not, that is the definition of consecration. If you want to have victory against the evil one, you must first make sure that your life has been set aside to be used by God. To do this is to consecrate our bodies, indeed our lives to be used by God. It makes sense to do this because after all, "...you are not your own. For you are bought with a price..." (1 Corinthians 6:19-20)

Notice that they were all *empty* vessels. That's the prerequisite for being used by God. Your vessel, that is, your life, has got to be empty. You've got to be willing to part with anything and everything that is a hindrance to being filled with the right thing. Now, you can't do that by yourself. It's not always an easy thing to do. Sometimes it's painful to part with those things that hinder God's unlimited work in your life. But take the risk and pray, "Search me, O God, and know my heart: try me, and know my thoughts: And see if there be any wicked way in me, and lead me in the way everlasting. (Psalm 139:23, 24 KJV) Gideon gave them empty pitchers or vessels. Gideon gave it to them empty because God wanted to fill them with something. If you skip ahead in the text, you will discover that Gideon gave them a torch or a light. Gideon then instructed them to take the light and put it in the vessel or pitcher. God wants to take out the trash and put in the light. God wants to take out the darkness and put in the light. God wants the vessel empty of anything that is not like God so that God can put in the light! So now, everyone has a trumpet, a vessel and inside of each vessel, a light.

Gideon then had the 300 men divided into three groups of 100 and ordered the men to surround the enemy's camp. It's late and the enemy is fast asleep. They do not expect Gideon and his army to come to their camp. Their arrogance and overconfidence will not let them conceive or consider such a thought. So they are sound asleep in their tents down in the valley.

Once Gideon and his men are in place surrounding the enemy's camp, Gideon blows the trumpet and his soldiers follow suit. When the enemy hears the noise they're startled. They are shaken from their slumber by an unanticipated declaration of War. To add to this sudden blare of trumpets, Gideon breaks his vessel and all of his men do the same. That means that not only does the additional sound add to the enemy's panic, but remember that every vessel has a light inside it. And once the vessel is broken, the lights are revealed surrounding the enemy's camp.

It's important to recognize the implications of this fact. The vessels have lights in them but in order for the enemy to see them, the vessels had to be broken. It is often true that God gets the brightest light from a broken vessel. Circumstances in life may seek to break you and even to destroy you. But God can take brokenness and use it to expose God's light within. Sometimes the light can't really be seen until we are sufficiently broken.

Which brings me to the third point: **the torch**. Gideon says to put a light in the vessels and break the vessel so the light will shine. That reminds me that Jesus said "Let your light so shine before men that they may see your good works and glorify the Father, which is in heaven." (Matthew 5:16) Notice that Jesus said *"let"* your light shine and not *"make"* your light shine. If he had said make your light shine then we might get confused and think that we are the source of the light. But we are not the source of the light we are just vessels carrying the light. God is the source of the light!

Well, once the vessels are broken and the Midianites immediately see 300 lights suddenly and simultaneously surrounding them, I am certain that amid the blaring noise and the camp wide panic, 300 lights must have seemed like 300,000!

But Gideon wasn't finished yet. Once they blew the trumpet, broke the vessels and revealed the light, Gideon told the men to **shout,** *"the sword of the Lord and of Gideon."* Did you catch that? Gideon told his men to shout! And that's good advice. That's what we have got to learn to do. Gideon didn't say "now once we win the victory I want you to shout." Gideon told them to shout before the victory. It was not only a shout in declaration of attack, it was a shout in *anticipation* of victory. This can remind us that often in the midst of the battles of life, we don't have to wait until the battle is over to shout. You can shout right now because you know that in the end you're going to win. You may be going through financial trouble but don't wait until you get out of debt to shout –shout right now! Your body may be sick, but don't wait until you're healed to shout; shout right now! Your marriage may be in trouble but don't wait until you reconcile to shout; shout right now! Your children may be in trouble but don't wait until they get out of trouble. I dare you to shout right now! I know it hurts, but shout. I know it is dark, but shout. Your heart may be filled with grief, but trust God and shout. The Bible says that God inhabits the praises of his people. When you shout, God shows up and when God shows up Satan steps back!

I know that shouting in church seems senseless to some folks. When I was growing up in the church we used to make fun of the old folks who "got happy" in church and shouted. We used to think that it was what ignorant, unlearned and unsophisticated folks did who weren't educated enough to handle some of life's tough troubles. But I have discovered that shouting, for our foreparents, was not the senseless expression of ignorant people. Shouting kept them sane. Shouting lifted their spirits. Shouting was both theological and therapeutic! Their shout was not a mere empty, emotive response to impossible circumstances. Sometimes the shout is the celebrative anticipation of divine breakthrough. The shout in the black church is not always the celebration of what has taken place, it is often the joyous affirmation of what we believe will take place. In the midst of overwhelming odds and intimidating obstacles, the shout was the declaration of the stubborn assurance in our spirit that "troubles do not last always". The shout was an unimpeded encounter with the Spirit, who then ministers to the spirit of the shouter the certainty that everything was going to be alright! The shout is today's response to tomorrow's victory. The shout is often anticipatory praise - not praise for what God did in the past or what God was doing in the present but what we believe God is going to do in the future. Gideon told his men to shout. And when they shouted the Bible says that the enemy turned on each other and began to self destruct. So if you believe that the victory is already yours, then in spite of the circumstances, in spite of the way things look, once you have done all that you know to do, go ahead and shout! God inhabits the praises of his people. And if God shows up in the praise, God can handle anything we've got to face. Go ahead and shout! Whatever your situation, pray your prayer, follow God's word, walk in faith, then go ahead and shout and watch the Lord give you the victory!

ABOUT THE AUTHOR

 Dr. F. Bruce Williams was born July 19, 1959 to Rev. Earl B. and Norrine T. Williams at Langley Air Force Base in Hampton, Virginia. Early in life, God ordained Dr. Williams' footsteps. Earning numerous honors, he graduated Summa Cum Laude from Florida A & M University and went on to obtain his Masters of Divinity from Southern Baptist Theological Seminary and his Doctorate in Ministry from the United Theological Seminary. Dr. Williams was installed as Senior Pastor of Bates Memorial Baptist Church, located in Smoketown, one of the poorest zip codes in Jefferson County, Louisville, Kentucky, in 1986 after serving as an associate minister. Twenty-five years later, the congregation has grown exponentially, seeing its membership increase from a hundred members to over five thousand members. Dr. Williams is committed to changing the lives of the marginalized, people that society has forgotten. The homeless, the drug addicts, the single mothers, the hurting and the suffering all have a purpose and a place in the Kingdom. Through his message of transformation and restoration, Dr. Williams encourages people to believe God, to believe in themselves, and to believe that there is something greater for their lives. He desires that all people seek after and discover their God-ordained purpose by introducing them to the power of the Savior. Dr. Williams is married to the former Leona Michelle Smith of Greensboro, Florida. Dr. F. Bruce and Dr. Michelle Williams are the proud parents of two daughters, Imani Colette and Nailah Cymone.

Also Available By Dr. F. Bruce Williams

<u>You Can Have As Far As You Can See</u>

You Can Have As Far as You Can See is a collection of inspirational and uplifting works penned by Dr. F. Bruce Williams, the pastor of Bates Memorial Baptist Church, located in Louisville, Kentucky. Ranging in topics on how to deal with your enemies, social justice, classic musings on a mother's love and the fight of a father to start all over again, *You Can Have As Far As You Can See* is a book that reaches out to all walks of life, with one common theme: it is never too late to embrace all that God has for you!

You Can Have As Far As You Can See teaches the reader not to be afraid to dream again. Don't be afraid to trust God for a new beginning. Don't be afraid to step out into unchartered territory with the expectation of experiencing the incredible. No, you don't know what your life holds. But you don't have to know; just go with God and believe, knowing that the choice is yours to possess all that God has in store for you!

CONTACT INFORMATION:
www.fbrucewilliamsministries.com
fbw@fbrucewilliamsministries.com

Bates Memorial Baptist Church
620 E. Lampton Street
Louisville, KY 40203

Made in the USA
Charleston, SC
27 May 2014